The Collectors Encyclopedia of

FLOW BLUE CHINA

Mary Frank Gaston

COLLECTOR BOOKS
A Division of Schroeder Publishing Co., Inc.

The current values in this book should be used only as a guide. They are not intended to set prices, which vary from one section of the country to another. Auction prices as well as dealer prices vary greatly and are affected by condition as well as demand. Neither the Author nor the Publisher assumes responsibility for any losses that might be incurred as a result of consulting this guide.

This Book is Dedicated
to the Memory of
my Father
FRANK BALLOW
1906-1982

Preface

For persons interested in antiques and collectables, the words "Flow Blue" bring to mind a very definite image. For new or beginning collectors, however, the words may not stand alone. These descriptive adjectives have become an important noun in today's general dictionary for antiques. Simply put, "Flow Blue" describes a category of blue and white decorated china where the blue color of the pattern "runs" onto the white background of the piece. The effect produced by this particular method of decorating china, which originated in England over one hundred and fifty years ago, is far more attractive than this definition implies. A muted, almost dreamy quality is imparted to designs applied in the "flown" manner. After seeing some examples of china decorated in that style, its appeal as well as its name is understood. It is also obvious why the word "china" does not have to be included for communication among collectors.

The United States is the principal place of interest for this category of antiques because so much was exported from England to American during the last century. Collector interest has greatly increased during the last few years. The age and beauty of these once very utilitarian and relatively inexpensive items continue to attract collectors although the prices of such pieces today far exceed those paid for such items ten or even five years ago. Today "Flow Blue" is considered a "Blue Chip" in the broad category of antique pottery and porcelain collecting. The value of the wares does not decrease over time for pieces in good condition, an important consideration for any type of collector.

Over four hundred photographs of Flow Blue are shown in this book. These photographs include over three hundred different patterns. It is not possible to show all of the Flow Blue patterns known to exist in this edition, of course. A large majority of these have been painstakingly detailed and documented in Petra Williams' books (see bibliography for complete references to her books). Quite a few patterns are shown here that are not in one of her books, but pattern identification is not the sole aim of this endeavor.

The purpose of this book is fourfold: First, to show all examples of Flow Blue in large full color photographs. Such photos help to point out better than words the intricacies of design of the many patterns, and thus we are fortunate in that the publisher thought all color photographs were important for this book.

The second intention is to show the marks found on examples to demonstrate the many different manufacturers of Flow Blue and the time period when the wares were made.

The third objective is to show a large variety of Flow Blue objects other than plates and bowls to point out the diverse items that were a part of day-to-day life during the last century.

The fourth purpose is to show the range of prices that Flow Blue patterns and objects command today. To do this, a separate Price Guide is included with this book. Price Guides are always controversial, but prices are asked, and more importantly, prices are paid for Flow Blue. Today's collector should be as knowledgeable as possible concerning the cost of such items. The information for the Price Guide is based on information compiled from collectors and dealers in order to reflect as accurate a price range as possible. The prices are intended to be used only as a guide.

I have traveled many miles to various locations to obtain the photographs for this book and to talk with collectors and dealers. As a result, I have been able not only to see lovely collections, but also to meet some very wonderful people. (Please see some of their names in the Acknowledgements). I hope you have as much pleasure seeing the examples of Flow Blue presented here as I did preparing this book. I hope that this work will serve to whet your appetite for continuing the study and collecting of FLOW BLUE!

Mary Frank Gaston
P.O. Box 342
Bryan, Texas 77806
Please include a SASE if a reply is requested.

4

Contents

Acknowledgements

I am extremely grateful to many people for their help in making this book possible. Collectors and dealers generously permitted me to photograph their collections and pieces which meant opening up their homes and disrupting their busy schedules, or rearranging their beautiful displays at shows, so that photographs could be made. They were all most kind and willing to help and share their knowledge about this subject with me. I would like to extend my thanks to these individuals:

Dorothy and Elmer Caskey, Covington, Ohio

Joyce Brown, Prairie Wind Antiques, Frederick, Oklahoma

Crawford's Antiques, San Antonio, Texas

Mr. and Mrs. Phil Cummins, Joshua, Texas

David Dodgen, Houston, Texas

Gladys M. Donham, Houston, Texas

Dunn & Ross Antiques, Houston, Texas

Arvena Fleury, O-P Book Shop and My House Antiques, #136, Trade Mart, Houston, Texas

Georgia Harris, Weathervane Antiques and Show Promotions, Columbus, Texas

Don and Charlene Johnson, Golden Age Antiques, Pawnee, Oklahoma

Professor and Mrs. William L. Hendricks, San Francisco, California

Suzanne King, Nottingham, England

Irene and Marc Luther

Vera McLeod, Curiosity Antique Shop, Big Spring, Texas

Lois Misiewicz, Fallbrook, California

Carolyn and Max Allen Nickerson, Nickerson's Antiques, Eldon, Missouri

Shirley Porter, The Antique Key, #40 & 41, Trade Mart, Houston, Texas

Connie Rogers, Dayton, Ohio

Lloyd Ward Antique Shows, Euless, Texas

Floris and Carl Walton, Grandfather's Trunk, Deland, Florida

Marceline White, The Chinaberry Tree, Stowell, Texas

Flow Blue items featured on the cover are also courtesy of Mr. and Mrs. Nickerson, Eldon, Missouri.

Last, but by no means least, I thank my husband and photographer, Jerry Gaston. Jerry has done all of the photography for my previous books, and this is, of course, no small task. In addition he takes me wherever I need to go to get the necessary information and photographs, plus he edits the manuscript and helps with the final stages of putting the book together. Needless to say, I am glad that he seems to enjoy this as much as I do. He is always the first to encourage me to go on to the next project!

Origins of Flow Blue

"There's a joy without
canker or cork
There's a pleasure
eternally new
Tis to gloat on the glaze
and the mark
Of china that's ancient
and blue."
Andrew Lang, from the
Ballad of Blue China

These words seem an apt description for collectors of one very interesting category of antiques--Flow Blue China. "Flow Blue" is the term used to describe ceramic items (semi-porcelain, stoneware, or porcelain) which have been decorated with blue underglaze designs and have a smudged or blurred appearance rather than a sharp, clear pattern. The blue color "bleeds" or "flows" onto the white body of the piece at the time the glaze decoration is fired in the kiln.

This particular method of decorating ceramics originated with potters located in the historic Staffordshire district of England sometime in the late 1820's. According to G. Bernard Hughes (*English and Scottish Earthenwares*, n.d.), Josiah Wedgwood II invented this technique of decoration. Hughes notes that certain chemical substances of saltpetre, borax and white lead were put in the saggers during the time of the "glost" (glaze) firing to achieve a "softer texture."

England became not only the first but the largest producer of this type of ware. Other European potters decorated in this manner to some extent later in the century. Also several potteries in the United States followed suit toward the end of the nineteenth century. Examples from these other countries as well as from England are included in this book.

The history of the Staffordshire pottery industry as well as the history of pottery and porcelain making and decorating in general, and in England, specifically, are indeed of interest to the collector. However, only a brief and fleeting glimpse of this industry as it relates to our subject, "Flow Blue" can be offered here. (Please see the Terms and Explanations section for relevant terms asociated with this industry and entries in the Bibliography for more detailed historical and technical information.)

"Flow Blue" was actually the consequence of two important inventions: Underglaze decoration and Transfer printing. Underglaze decoration is superior to overglaze decoration because the pattern is sealed so to speak and cannot be worn off through time or through use. Handpainted

underglaze decoration in blue had been used by the Chinese on porcelain for centuries. The decoration was blue because that was the one color the Chinese had discovered that would tolerate the high temperatures required to fire a glaze on a ceramic body. The color was obtained from the mineral, cobalt. Chinese blue and white decorated porcelain had been exported to England as early as the 1600's. Attempts to emulate this type of decoration were not successful, however, until the next century. When the English potters were able to obtain this cobalt color, the majority of which had to be imported from Saxony, English ceramics could also have underglaze handpainted blue decoration. Handpainted decoration was, of course, attractive and was especially desirable once such decoration could be applied under the glaze. However, handpainted designs still required a lot of time because each item had to be decorated individually.

Toward the middle of the 1700's the process of transfer printing was invented. (See the Terms and Explanations section for a definition of this process.) Transfer printing allowed the same design to be used over and over again. It was quicker and cheaper than handpainted decoration. Before underglaze decoration was possible, transfer patterns were applied over the glaze on ceramic bodies. They too, like handpainted overglaze designs, showed signs of wear and use through time. Once the technique for underglaze decoration was found to be possible by using this substance obtained from cobalt, the door was opened for decorating with blue transfer printed patterns underglaze as well as handpainted underglaze designs.

The Worcester factory is considered to be the first to accomplish underglaze transfer printing on porcelain bodies in the 1760's. Thomas Turner at the Caughley works is usually credited with being the first, circa 1780, to use transfer designs underglaze on earthenware bodies. It is important to note that it was necessity, not choice, that caused the first underglaze transfer patterns to be in blue rather than in some other color. During the first quarter of the nineteenth century, blue underglaze transfer designs were firmly established as a decorating technique. By the mid 1800's, it was also possible to use colors other than blue underglaze.

The combination of underglaze decoration and transfer printing revolutionized the English ceramic industry. When these processes were perfected, ceramics could be decorated quickly, efficiently, and inexpensively. Attractive patterns with elaborate detail could be applied to all manner of tablewares and accessories, making matched sets possible and also affordable for the mass population.

Flow Blue was also born as a result of these processes. The first blue underglaze transfer patterns were not Flow Blue, but Flow Blue was a direct result of these techniques. The transfer patterns had to be applied in sections on the borders and sides of objects. If the process was not done correctly, the seams where the sections were joined were quite noticeable and of course not attractive. Therefore the technique of causing the blue color to flow during the glaze firing was first used as a means of hiding such decorating faults and to thus keep the design from having such an obvious "transfer" look. Eventually, the result of this decorating technique became popular itself for this "flown" look, and manufacturers produced wares decorated in this manner for their decorative appeal. Later patterns in colors other than blue were made using this "flow" technique.

The peak years for the production of English Flow Blue were from the middle 1800's through the early 1900's. Increased industrialization of the potteries allowing mass production of wares and the refinement of the underglaze transfer printing process were, of course, primary factors for the growth of the English ceramic industry as a whole as well as for the production of Flow Blue. But perhaps just as important was the export trade with America developed by the English pottery industry. The American market was quite keen for this type of ware long after it had lost its appeal in England. It is evident from the many manufacturers' names on the back stamps of examples that not just a few, but literally hundreds of English potters produced Flow Blue. The English potters did their best to satisfy the tremendous export demand. If the demand had not been so great in America, it is highly unlikely that such a large amount of Flow Blue would have been produced.

Collecting Flow Blue

The United States has become the center for collecting Flow Blue, and that is not surprising. Although the majority of Flow Blue was made in England, the English do not attach as much antique value to this type of ware, perhaps because it was inexpensive, mass produced, and transfer decorated. Another obvious reason is that there is not a large supply available in England today if collectors were interested. This is a result of it being largely an export product during the last century, and because of American interest arising during the latter half of this century which has caused vast lots to be culled from England to be sold to collectors in the United States. Upon hearing that I was working on a book about Flow Blue, a friend of mine in England said she would treat her large Flow Blue platter, which she uses without thought to its age or value, more carefully now! The same thing is true in other areas of collecting such as Nippon, R.S. Prussia, and Limoges. These porcelains were manufactured primarily for export, and today collector interest is in this country rather than Japan, Germany, or France. Additionally, collectors must have access to items to collect. As America is a "youngster" by European standards, it has not been possible for most of us to concentrate on collections of any type of great antiquity.

Many examples of Flow Blue, however, are considered true antiques, because they are over a hundred years old. I think that this particular age factor is a primary motivation for many Flow Blue collectors because it allows us to touch history. In addition to age and availability, a large selection of different types of pieces, a wide range of patterns and styles of decoration, plus a host of manufacturers combine to give Flow Blue an inherent facility for collectability.

Objects

A quick look at the Object Index in this book will give an indication of the assortment of Flow Blue wares that were manufactured. These items were a necessary part of life for people during this primarily Victorian era in history. Most of the items come under the categories of tablewares or personal accessories (dresser items and wash sets). Such pieces were inexpensive when made and were intended for every day use. However, many of the "necessary" items of that time are considered "rare" today, basically because of their scarcity. The pieces were used, thus they became chipped, cracked, and broken through time. So a wash basin, a toothbrush holder, or a chamber pot (and especially its lid) are scarce today. In tablewares, more plates and bowls were made than serving or condiment pieces. Thus cheese dishes, egg holders, and tureens for example are rare, as are cups, which seem to be the first to go from every set of dishes!

Art or decorative items in Flow Blue such as vases, portrait or wall plaques, and jardinieres are also more rare than tablewares because fewer of these types of pieces were manufactured. Many of these types of items were also manufactured more toward the latter part of the history of the industry. Miniatures and children's dishes are other scarce categories of Flow Blue.

Not only the type of object, but the mold design and body shape of those objects are of collector interest. Look at the shape of an object without regard to its pattern or color. You will see that a plate, for instance, may be completely round in shape, or scalloped, or composed of many sides (panelled). It may also be nearly flat or have a rather deep well. A bowl may be completely curved or have a wide outer flange. Hollowwares (cups, teapots, pitchers, etc.) may have smooth spherical shapes or definite sides. Their bases and borders may also be sided, round, or scalloped. Their handles, feet, and finials may be straight, simply curved, or elaborately formed with curved and twisted shapes. Swirled scroll shapes or floral motifs may appear as decoration on the bodies of all types of pieces.

These diverse body shapes give the items a unique appearance and add diversity and interest to a collection. These same qualities may also indicate the particular time period the pieces were made. Sided and plainly shaped items are considered older than those with rounded or scalloped shapes. Ornate molded body designs as well as fancy handles and finials are considered later than those more plainly designed.

Methods and Patterns of Decoration

The "flowing" look is, of course, the main point of differentiation between Flow Blue and other blue and white decorated ceramics. The "flow" may vary from very dark to quite faint. It may cover the entire surface of the piece or be confined to only the outer border. The degree of darkness of the blue is sometimes thought to be the main criterion of age, for the early blue printing was very dark. However through time, lighter shades of blue were perfected and desired. During the period when most of the examples we see today were made, it was posible to "flow" the patterns in various shades of blue.

As we have noted, the patterns were either handpainted or applied as transfer designs. Some handpainted designs were made in a definite, though usually simple, pattern such a vines, leaves, or floral shapes. Other handpainted wares just exhibited gradations of the flowing color or colored molded designs on the body of the piece. Copper lustre or other colors applied over the glaze are also seen on hand-painted examples. Basically handpainted Flow Blue comes from the early period of the industry, and most examples are usually unmarked.

Transfer decoration was used as the primary method of decorating Flow Blue. Intricate borders and elaborate center patterns were possible with this method. Look close-ly at the various components in a border pattern. The many different designs composing the pattern often seem to defy description. However the overall design will have a main point of characterization, details that are repeated so that it is possible to distinguish it from another pattern. Geometric, scroll, and floral shapes categorize most Flow Blue border patterns. Sometimes scenic or figural cameos are featured on the borders, often repeating the center pat-tern. Other examples may have only bands of color on the border, and some pieces do not have any border at all.

Some Flow Blue patterns have only a border pattern, but the majority also have a center pattern. The center patterns may repeat or enlarge the chief characteristic of the border pattern, or it may be entirely different from the border. Some Flow Blue manufacturers made two versions of the same pattern: one with only a border and the other with a border and a center pattern. The size and shape of pieces often determined how much of a pattern could be applied to a piece. Therefore, cups and butter pats, for instance, may have only partial patterns of their large matching counterparts such as plates and platters. In other cases, the patterns are replicated but scaled down to size to fit the piece.

The decorative themes of the patterns found on Flow Blue are numerous and varied and reflect the popular ar-tistic tastes of the times when the pieces were made. We know that the very first underglaze patterns sought to emulate the Chinese designs. This oriental influence was carried on during the early days of Flow Blue production. Later patterns depicted figural and scenic designs of a historical or romantic nature, and of course floral patterns were very popular. Animal, bird, and portrait themes are found to a lesser extent.

Some of the Flow Blue transfer patterns were polychrom-ed over the glaze. Such pieces are quite attractive if the hand applied color has not become worn off through time or use. Gold trim or gold spattered work is another attrac-tive embellishment on some Flow Blue items. Overglaze enamelling, usually on the borders, was used also as add-ed decoration for some patterns.

The prolific manufacturers of Flow Blue were not con-tent to make the wares in just a few patterns, or even just a few hundred patterns. A minimum estimate would be that over 1500 different Flow Blue patterns were made during the relatively long period of its production. The majority of the transfer decorated pieces have a pattern name on the back or base of the object. This sounds good because so many other types of European table wares from this same time era did not have pattern names marked on them. As a result, involved systems must be designed to classify such patterns for collectors of those products today. Therefore Flow Blue collectors do have a definite advan-tage in this respect, but identifying Flow Blue patterns by the pattern name that is stamped on them is not always as straightforward as it sounds. The reason is because many companies used the same patterns. As a result, one finds examples of the same pattern with different manufac-turer's marks. That is not so bad if the patterns are the same and marked with the same pattern name. But the same patterns often have entirely different names as well as different manufacturers. Additionally some pattern names were used by many different companies, but the pat-terns are not the same–only the pattern name. Occasionally one also finds that one company gave the same pattern name to more than one design. Sometimes in these latter instances, the borders of the patterns may be the same, but the center designs are different, but in some cases the pat-terns are completely different. It is very likely that mistakes were made in marking the pieces with the wrong pattern name through haste or carelessness which resulted in this form of duplication.

The Staffordshire potters and other Flow Blue manufac-turers did not intentionally set out to give today's collec-tors a headache when they duplicated Flow Blue pattern names and patterns. The basic reason for this duplication was a result of the transfer printing process. Once this pro-cedure was perfected, engraving patterns for use on ceramics became a business itself.

Thomas Minton left the Caughley works to become a master engraver in London. He sold his patterns to various potteries as did other engravers. The purchasers could do what they pleased with the transfers. They could use the name that the pattern might have been given, or they could decide on their own name for the pattern. They could also print the pattern with or without the "flow" technique, and in colors other than blue (after it was possible to use other colors underglaze). The makers had no idea that the wares they were making and naming would eventually be of an-tique or historical interest. They were making the dishes for the present as quickly and cheaply as they could. It did not matter if more than one company called the same pat-tern the same name, or a different name, or if they called entirely different patterns the same name.

In other instances, we find that when one company took over another, the pattern names were continued although the manufacturer's mark might change. "Seville" by New Wharf and "Seville" by Wood and Son are the same pat-tern and were made at the same factory, but some examples have one company name and some another, because Wood and Son purchased the New Wharf Pottery. The chronology of this form of successvie ownership or "changing hands" in the English pottery industry is well documented by God-den and helps to clarify some of the duplications of pat-terns and company marks found on Flow Blue.

It is interesting just to browse through a list of Flow Blue pattern names, regardless of manufacturer's mark. Rivers, towns, states, and countries of the world as well as proper names and terms for flowers and plants are some of the broad categories into which the pattern names may be classified. Sometimes the name relates to the picture on the face of the pieces, often it does not. Because a particular flower appears to be the main feature of a pattern, that does not necessarily mean that the pattern name is the name of that flower; likewise if the pattern name is a proper name such as Janette or Florida, that does not mean that the design features a girl or anything remotely connected with the state of Florida! Personally, I think that the persons responsible for naming the patterns probably greatly enjoyed their work in concocting names they thought might interest and thus entice buyers of the wares!

Some pieces of Flow Blue do not have a pattern name marked on them. However, the reasons for this are not what is commonly thought. It is sometimes believed that the early pieces were not marked because the custom of marking names of patterns on pieces had not been established. However, pattern names were regularly in use in England after 1820 when Flow Blue was first being made. The custom was in practice, but it was not a requirement. Therefore some firms evidently saw no reason to mark their products with pattern names, or were not systematic in their marking procedures, because identical pieces can be found both marked and unmarked.

Marks

Manufacturer's marks found on Flow Blue are a study in themselves. It is rewarding to track down or identify the company that made a particular piece in one's possession. Why is this? Why do we almost always look at the back or base of a piece to see what mark, if any, is on it? Basically we want to know how old the piece might be. Usually we can only hope to know this from the mark on the piece. If it is marked, we can look in references on marks to see if that particular mark or company is identified, and if so when that company was in business or when that particular type of mark was used by the company. In some categories of pottery and porcelain collecting, the information we do find is rather general and thus disappointing. "Nineteenth century" for example is not really too helpful as a time period, except to designate that the piece is not new. But because of the record keeping of many producers of all types of ceramic products, this type of dating is often as close as we can come to knowing the history of a particular piece.

Flow Blue collectors are fortunate because so many pieces were marked with manufacturer's marks as well as pattern marks. Most importantly, the majority of English pottery and porcelain manufacturers has been exceedingly well documented, especially by Geoffrey Godden (*Encyclopedia of British Pottery and Pottery Marks*, 1964) and J.P. Cushion (*Handbook of Pottery and Porcelain Marks*, 1980). Collectors of all types of English ceramics are able to date many of their pieces more precisely than just to a broad time period.

As a result of such available information, marks are the best source for dating examples of Flow Blue. They are more reliable in most instances even than the shape, color

(or depth or shade of color), or theme of decoration. It is important to remember, however, that the majority of dates for these manufacturers still encompass certain time periods. If a certain mark is noted to have been used from 1840 to 1875, for example, we know that the piece was not made before 1840 or after 1875. However, we can seldom say that the piece was made in 1855 just because that date falls between those years. It should be emphasized that pieces can rarely be dated to an exact year. Some companies such as Davenport, Minton, and Wedgwood at certain periods did use various marking systems to show specific years of manufacture. The majority of companies, however, did not. For those that did, references provide keys to decipher these marks.

Caution should also be used in interpreting English registry marks. These marks are encountered on many examples of Flow Blue. References provide tables for decoding these marks, but such marks do not indicate the year that a specific piece was made. (For more about this, see "Registry Mark" in the Terms and Explanations section.)

Most of the marks on Flow Blue were made from transfer designs and applied under the glaze rather than being incised or impressed. Such printed marks could be quite elaborate containing symbols and words pertaining to the name and location of the company. Frequently marks included the specific term the manufacturer used to designate the ceramic body of his ware, such as "semi-porcelain," "stoneware," and so forth. The information in the marks also often aids in determining the time periods specific marks were used. It is important to note if marks contain such words as "Son," "Co.," "Ltd.," or more than one name or set of initials. Usually such wording reflected a change in the status of the firm, and references note the time or time period when such changes went into effect.

These underglaze marks cannot be taken off or worn off thorugh time; thus, there is no doubt that the mark was put on at the time the piece was made. However, because of the "flowing" process, many of the underglaze marks are impossible to read, for they too became "flown." In some instances makers of pieces with illegible marks or unmarked examples can be discovered by matching the pattern and shape to other marked examples. This is not always possible though because companies used the same types of molds as well as the same patterns. But if the pattern and shape of the pieces, one marked and one unmarked, are identical, the specific company that made the unmarked piece is not usually of great importance when one is wanting to match or complete a set of a certain pattern.

Because of so many variations in Flow Blue patterns and marks, it is easy to see that as much information as possible should be given if one is trying to match a particular pattern or object. Size, shape, pattern name, and manufacturer's mark are all desirable pieces of information. Pictures of the piece and its mark are perhaps the most helpful clues of all.

Useful Terms and Explanations for Flow Blue

There are some basic terms that are important for collectors to know, especially beginning collectors, which are pertinent to the study and appreciation of Flow Blue. Some of these basic terms with brief definitions are explained in this section, arranged alphabetically within three categories: Ceramics, Decoration, and Marks.

Ceramics

Biscuit denotes items made of clay, earthenwares or porcelains, which have been fired only once and are unglazed.

Bisque is the same as "Biscuit" except it is almost always used to refer to unglazed hard paste porcelain rather than earthenware.

Body is the form of an object.

Bone China is a type of pottery composed of at least 50% bone ash, the calcined bones of animals. It is translucent, but is not considered true or hard paste porcelain. Bone china was invented by Josiah Spode I in the late 1700's.

Ceramic means items composed of clay and fired at high temperatures.

China popularly refers to any kind of ceramic body, such as "Flow Blue China." Its true definition means hard paste porcelain.

Crazing refers to thin lines that appear on the glazed surface of earthenwares which in turn allow the glaze to be penetrated. Crazing is caused by age and heat. It results because the body and glaze of an object were not fired at high enough temperatures to become completely vitrified.

Earthenware technically is one of the two classes of pottery. Earthenwares have a porosity of more than 50%. They are composed of various types of natural clays and fired at high temperatures. They are opaque and not vitreous, although they may be glazed as most examples are. Bricks and flower pots are examples of unglazed earthenware.

Embossed designates a slightly raised design used to decorate the body of an object. Embossed designs are formed from the clay paste of the object before the piece is ever fired.

Finial is a decoration applied to the tops or lids of ceramic items. These are made from the same materials as the body of the piece.

Fired means to bake clay formed items at high temperatures.

Hollowware refers to molded ceramic items that are "hollow" or "open" with a definite "inside" space such as pitchers and sugar bowls, etc., as opposed to flatware such as plates.

Ironstone is a form of stoneware where ground iron slag has been mixed with the clay. Ironstone was patented in 1813 in England by Mason.

Mold (or **Mould**) is a form made in a desired shape to hold the clay paste and thus give form to the object.

Molded means to shape the body paste to give form to an object, either by hand or in a prepared mold.

Opaque is the opposite of translucent and means that you cannot see through the object.

Panelled refers to ceramic bodies which are molded with definite sides rather than being totally round and smooth in shape.

Paste is the clay composition of a ceramic body before it is fired. It more commonly refers to hard paste or soft paste porcelain.

Porcelain is technically a form of stoneware because it is fired to a state of vitrification, however porcelain is distinguished from stoneware because porcelain is translucent. The term "porcelain" is used to designate true or hard paste porcelain whose principal ingredient is kaolin, a type of clay containing hydrated aluminum silicates.

Pottery refers to objects formed from clay and fired at high temperatures. The two major categories of Pottery are earthenwares and stonewares.

Relief means raised ceramic decoration which stands out from the body of the object, shaped or applied before the object is fired.

Rococo applies to ornately shaped ceramic bodies often having fancy embossed or relief designs on the body as well.

Sagger is the ceramic box that holds the objects in the kiln during the firing proces.

Scalloped is a semi-circular shape, usually referring to the outer edge of ceramic items. The term originated from the shell of a scallop.

Semi-Porcelain means any glazed earthenware pottery. It is opaque and not vitreous.

Soft Paste refers to a type of porcelain. Soft paste porcelain is fired at lower temperatures than hard paste porcelain. Originally soft paste porcelain was made in an attempt to imitate Chinese hard paste porcelain. The word "soft" refers to the temperatures used and does not describe the texture of the wares.

Spur Marks are the marks left by the clay supports that were used to separate plates and bowls during the firing process. The marks are small protrusions usually found in three places either on the back or front of the pieces.

Stilt Marks are the same as spur marks.

Stoneware technically is the second major classification of pottery. Stonewares have a porosity of less than 5% because feldspar and quartz are added to the clay mixture, and they are fired at high enough temperatures to become vitrified. This is accomplished in the first firing. Stonewares are not fired to a state of translucency, however.

Translucent is the opposite of opaque and means that you can see through the object. Translucency is the chief characteristic of porcelain.

Vitreous refers to the glass-like quality given to ceramic bodies by glazes fired on those bodies. Stonewares and porcelains are completely vitreous because the glaze and the body are fired until the body and glaze become one entity, and thus the outer glaze cannot be penetrated. Earthenwares, though, are not fired at temperatures high enough to make the body and glaze one entity. The glazes on earthenwares are vitreous, that is glass-like, but they can be penetrated. That is why the glazes on earthenwares craze.

Well means the middle part inside the rim or border of ceramic flatware such as the well of a plate.

Decoration

Chinoisiere refers to decoration emulating Chinese styles.

Cobalt is an ore found in copper, silver, or tin mines.

Cobalt Blue is a color used to decorate ceramics obtained from an oxide of the mineral, cobalt. The substance is brown in color when it is applied to the ceramic body, but the high heat during the firing process transforms the color to a deep blue.

Copper Lustre is a metallic glaze made from copper which has an irridescent look.

Enamelled refers to handpainted raised decoration applied over the glaze on ceramic bodies. Such decoration often outlines designs in the pattern.

Gilded means to decorate with gold.

Glaze refers to the liquid, glassy substance which is applied to ceramics to make them impervious to liquids, and also used in various colors to decorate ceramics.

Glost has the same meaning as glaze.

Monochrome means that only one color is used to decorate an object.

Motif refers to the theme of decoration of an object, such as floral.

Overglaze designates that the decoration has been applied after an object has been glazed and fired.

Polychromed means that more than one color is used to decorate an object.

Slip refers to a liquid form of clay used for decorating.

Theme applies to the dominant subject characterizing the decoration, such as scenic theme or floral theme.

Transfer Decoration means that designs or patterns have been engraved on copper plates, the grooves of the design filled with paint, after which the copper plate is heated and a soapy tissue paper is pressed into the engraved design, taken off and in turn pressed upside down on an object which has been heated and coated with varnish. After the object has dried, the paper is washed off, but the design remains--thus the design has been "transferred" from the copper plate to this object.

Underglaze designates decoration applied before an object has been glazed and fired.

Marks

"England" is found in some English marks from the last quarter of the nineteenth century, but was used on all exported wares after 1891 to comply with American tariff laws.

Garter Mark is a printed mark, round or oval in shape, used in English marks during the latter half of the nineteenth century. See "Cauldon" in the Marks section for one example.

Impressed marks are made in the form of initials or symbols and pressed into the ceramic body before it is fired. See Minton for an example.

Incised marks are cut into the ceramic body before it is fired.

Limited (LTD.) is a word or abbreviation found in many English marks after 1880.

"Made In England" is noted by most authorities to be definitely of twentieth century origin, but such a mark does not specifically date from any one year, and its use was not required; thus some examples from the same historical period may have this mark and others will not.

Overglaze describes marks placed on an object after it has been glazed. Overglaze marks are handpainted or printed. Marks applied overglaze can be worn off or taken off.

Printed Marks refer to marks made in the form of a transfer or stamp. Such marks can be applied either over or under the glaze.

Raised means marks formed in relief and applied to the piece.

Registry Marks (RD.) are marks or numbers impressed or printed on English ceramics after 1842. Diamond shaped marks were the first type used and continued until 1883. After that time the consecutive numbering system, prefaced with the initials "RD" was used. Tables to decipher such marks are found in general marks books. These registration numbers were assigned to companies in order to protect a shape or pattern design for three years. When interpreted, these letters or numbers will tell you the year that such designs were first registered, but that does not mean that your example with a certain registry mark was made on the day of the month of a certain year or even a certain year. The marks were continued after the three year period. Thus they only tell you when the company registered the design, and it is possible that they used the design before they registered it. Many designs, of course, were never registered.

"Royal" is a word used in English marks after 1850.

Staffordshire Knot refers to a bow-knot shape used to mark English ceramics during the 1880's. See "New Wharf Pottery" for an example.

"Trade Mark" is a term used in English marks primarily after the last quarter of the nineteenth century.

Underglaze refers to marks applied to ceramic bodies before they are glazed. Such marks are permanent and cannot be worn or taken off (although, of course, they can be covered over).

Trends and Prospects

Prior to the 1970's Flow Blue had a relative steady or stable collector interest. Collectors and dealers recognized the pieces as old and of English origin, and blue and white patterns on any type of china have always been considered attractive and thus popular. Premium value, however, was not usually assigned to Flow Blue wares prior to the 1970's. With regard to antique ceramics, the higher values were placed on porcelains rather than on earthenwares and stonewares of the same vintage.

The 1970's, though, witnessed a rapid growth in antiques and collectables of all sorts brought about largely through increased exposure of such items through a rising number of antique shows, flea markets, and auctions becoming popular throughout the United States, plus a larger number of books and price guides being published on all areas of collector interest. Flow Blue benefited from this exposure and was especially stimulated by Petra Williams' books on the subject. Her books on Flow Blue pattern identification gave the topic excellent visibility. As a result of increased interest, the number of Flow Blue collectors has greatly increased--much to the chagrin of earlier collectors, perhaps, because prices are now quite high and examples are becoming scarce especially for popular patterns and unusual pieces. One knowledgeable dealer in the field told me that supplies were becoming so scarce on the East coast (where Flow Blue had been relatively plentiful), that he doubted if he would be able to offer a very large or diverse assortment in the next few years.

But as awareness and interest has led to increased collecting or even "hoarding" in some instances, at least the desirability of Flow Blue and thus its future as a field of antique or collector interest has become assured. Therefore, it will not just gradually disappear from the market. It will still be possible to buy and sell the wares as they surface through time at estate and auction sales and make their way back to the marketplace. However, because of the niche Flow Blue has made for itself in the category of antique pottery and porcelain, it is very unlikely that yesteryears' prices will ever return for these wares!

Objects are collected because of age, uniqueness, or scarcity. Sometimes items have all of these three characteristics. Historically, Flow Blue was collected for its age and its unique decoration characteristic of the "flowing" color, and more recently because of its scarcity. Production of Flow Blue did not automatically cease by all manufacturers at one specific point in time. It is apparent, from looking at the dates shown for the marks found on pieces in this book, that many examples were made during the early 1900's, and some produced even after 1930. These later pieces are also very collectable, especially as the older ones become scarce. However, I think that most collectors and dealers would agree that one should be able to say that antique or collectable Flow Blue should be considered as products made prior to 1940 at the outside. I am sure that advanced collectors would probably say that 1900 or 1920 would be a better cut-off date, but advanced collectors do not have to be too concerned with arbitrary cut-off dates. The beginning collector is the one more likely to be concerned, because they want to be sure that they are indeed buying the "real" thing.

Some of today's new collectors may occasionally get burned if they have not become familiar with marks and decoration of the genuine article. For several years now, new Flow Blue has been manufactured by at least one firm in England. The Blakeney Pottery Limited, located at Stoke-on-Trent, has been in business since 1968. Their advertising notes that the wares were originally made for the American market. The objects are termed "Victorian Reproductions," and are made in the form of mustache cups, shaving mugs, wash basins, pitchers, hatpin holders, and dresser trays to name a few. Large blue roses make up the pattern on these pieces. The items are marked with a coat of arms and "Victoria" which is apparently used as a pattern name. See Plates 435 and 436 for photographs of this mark and an example of the ware.

Cushion shows some other marks for this company. To date I have not seen examples with these other marks. Two are in the shape of garter marks, one round, the other oval, both with a crown and a ribbon with the name "Victoria" printed on it. Another mark is in the form of a large floral cartouche. "Romantic" is printed inside this mark evidently designating another pattern name, and "Flo Blue, T.M. Staffordshire, England" is printed underneath the mark.

The examples I have seen of these new or modern pieces really pose no problem and are easily recognizable as a new product to the trained collector's eye. The company's advertising, however, says that the items are as near to the 1870 Flow Blue ware as they can obtain with contemporary materials. The pieces are not expensive when purchased from the wholesaler or even the majority of the retailers who sell these articles. Most examples are commonly seen at flea markets and even some antique shops. Some sellers do try to pass the pieces off as old, or if one wants to be charitable, one can say perhaps the person is uninformed. For example, at a booth in an antique mall, a dealer had one of the shaving mugs. It was priced at over one hundred dollars. I inquired if the piece was "old" and was told, "of course." Evidence strongly suggests that these wares have been sold as the genuine article.

Another new Flow Blue piece is shown in Plate 434. It is a mold copy of the vase in Plate 370, differing only in that the new vase has had fancy handles applied. There is no manufacturer's mark on this piece, although it was noted by the owner to have come from North Carolina. The decoration is a far superior "Flow Blue" than the other contemporary piece shown in Plate 436, and is more likely to fool the untrained eye.

It is likely that other new Flow Blue will appear on the market in the future basically because of the prices that the old and geniune pieces are now commanding. This always happens, it seems, when prices reach three figures. The best protection is to be as knowledgeable as possible through study about and contact with the "old" Flow Blue, and to be alert for such new items.

Introduction to Photographs

The photographs in this book are divided into Manufacturers' Marks and examples of Flow Blue. The Marks are presented first and are numbered consecutively. These Marks and numbers are referred to in the photographs of Flow Blue. English marks are arranged alphabetically by company. Dates for those marks are included in the mark's caption. Information on dates is based either on Geoffrey Godden's *Encyclopedia of British Pottery and Porcelain Marks* (1964) or on J.P. Cushion's *Handbook of Pottery and Porcelain Marks (1980)*.

In some instances, the precise marks on the pieces I photographed were not shown in those books, but beginning and closing dates for the firms were noted. That tells us that a particular mark could not have been used before or after those dates. It is also very important to note that marks could change in appearance only slightly by using "Son," "Limited," and so forth; so in interpreting "circa" dates of the marks, I have followed such small variations in dating the specific marks photographed.

Please remember that I show only the marks found on pieces shown in the photographs--not all of one company's various marks. It is possible that your specific piece may have a mark different from the mark I show, especially some small variation such as listed above. To show all possible mark variations would be impossible, therefore you may wish to consult Godden or Cushion for detailed information of company histories and their other marks.

Many of the English marks have pattern names either inside the mark or adjacent to the mark. Disregard the pattern name when looking at my marks. For example, I show over 30 patterns on pieces made by Grindley, but I show only three different Grindley marks. In the photographs of pieces with Grindley patterns, I refer you to one of the three marks; however, the photograph of the mark will have either (1) Marechal Neil, (2) Marguerite, or (3) Beauty Roses as a pattern name contained in the mark. But one of those three marks will be referred to in the captions of the photographs of all the other pictures of Grindley patterns. It would be redundant to present the same Grindley mark over and over again when only the pattern name is different.

In the English Marks section, several marks containing various initials remain unidentified, but they are included. They are arranged in alphabetical order by first initial. Some other unidentified symbols are also shown at the end of the English Marks section. The English Marks are followed by Non-English Marks, including U.S. manufacturers, and are arranged alphabetically by country of origin and within country by manufacturer.

Next, photographs of Flow Blue are divided into four groups. The first is for English Flow Blue, arranged alphabetically by pattern name. The pattern names are shown in all capital letters. The name of the manufacturer, where known, and the mark used by that manufacturer are indicated by a Mark Number which corresponds to a photograph in the Marks section. In some instances, the mark was too illegible for printing, so there is not a corresponding mark number, however, the mark that was on the piece is described in the caption.

In a few cases, the pieces photographed did not have a pattern name marked on them. A popular name, however, is associated with those patterns, and that popular name is used to identify the pattern. COWS and GEORGE WASHINGTON are examples of such popular names.

Some other pieces I photographed also did not have a pattern name marked on them, and no obvious popular name was associated with those patterns. However, some of these patterns appeared to match a pattern in one of Petra Williams' books. In such cases, I show the pattern name in quotation marks with only the first letter capitalized. The caption for that pattern refers the reader to a specific page in one of Williams' books in order to compare my example with the one she shows under that particular pattern name. For example, see Plate 82. This piece did not have a pattern name marked on it, but it seems to match the pattern shown as "Dahlia" on page 96 of Williams' Book I.

Some of these examples without pattern names marked on them did have a company name marked on them, but some did not. If there was a company mark, it may or may not have been the same company name or mark that Williams notes for that pattern. Therefore, if my example had a company mark, I indicate that it did in the caption. If it did not have a company name marked on it, I show that it did not by saying "unmarked" in the caption. Because so many manufacturers used the same patterns, we cannot always definitely say who the manufacturer was. But if we can say that the pattern is the same as that of one company, that is better than saying that the pattern is unidentified or making up a name for it.

The second group of Flow Blue photographs is of pieces that neither had a pattern name stamped on them, a popular name associated with them, nor appeared to match a pattern in any of Williams' books. The section is titled "Unidentified Patterns" and is arranged alphabetically by type of object. I have not attempted to make up names for these patterns because examples may show up later with a pattern name. Also the name I could suggest may not be the best term to describe the pattern. The numbers of the photographs can be used to identify these examples to interested buyers and sellers.

The third group of photographs is of Handpainted Flow Blue items. These pieces did not have pattern names marked on them, and because I encountered more than one popular name for some of these patterns, I decided that it was best for collectors simply to use my photograph numbers to identify these handpainted patterns.

The fourth group of photographs is of Non-English Flow Blue pieces. These are products of other European countries and the United States. The photographs are arranged alphabetically by country. Pattern names are shown only if the example had a pattern name marked on it, or if a popular name is associated with the pattern. For example, "La Belle" is a designation for a particular line of china manufactured by the Wheeling Pottery Company of Wheeling, West Virginia. The name "La Belle" was used on different themes of decoration on the company's wares, but collectors and dealers use "La Belle" as the name specifically for one floral pattern made by that firm. For Non-English Flow Blue examples without marked pattern names or popular names, the photograph numbers also can be used to identify those patterns.

Several indexes are provided to aid in locating companies and patterns and objects. Please note that there is not an index of English patterns because the photographs of those patterns are presented alphabetically. However, there are indexes for Non-English patterns, English Manufacturers and their Patterns, Non-English Manufacturers (arranged alphabetically by country), Manufacturer's Initials, Ambiguous Marks, and Types of Objects.

English Manufacturers and Their Patterns

Adams, William & Son: Berlin Groups, Jeddo
Adams, William & Co.: Fairy Villas, Garland, Geisha, Gloria, Kyber, Mazura; see also Plate 362
Adams, W. & T.: Asiatic Pheasants
Alcock, Henry: Bouquet, Manhattan, Touraine
Alcock, J. & G.: Circassia, Scinde
Alcock, Samuel & Co.: Kremlin
Allerton, Charles & Sons: Plate 389
Allertons: Mabel
Ashworth, G. L. & Bros.: Hizen, Vista, Yedo
Bishop & Stonier: Khan, Lancaster
Bourne & Leigh: Chinese, Florentine, Ophir
Brown-Westhead, Moore & Co.: Breadlebane
Burgess & Leigh: Burleigh, Celeste, Italia, Non Pareil, Raleigh, Vermont, Windflower; see also Plate 379
Cauldon: Candia; see also Plate 368
Challinor, Edward: Pelew
Clark, Edward & Co.: Lucania
Clementson & Young: Tonquin
Colley, Alfred, Ltd.: Lusitania
Corn, W. & E.: Ayr, Dorothy, Flannel Daisy, Iris
Davenport: Amoy
Dean, S.W.: Blossom
Dimmock, Thomas: Chinese
Doulton & Co.: Beverly, Buttercup, Geneva, Gibson Girl, George Washington, Glorie de Dijon, Madras, Martha Washington, Melrose, Norbury, Vernon, Virginia Watteau, Willow: see also Plates 332, 348, 355, 359, 363, 377
E.W.: Chinese Plant
Edwards, T.: Cabul
Fell, Thomas: Excelsior
Ford & Sons: Argyle, Bristol, Geisha, Milan, Oxford, Ruskin, Sandon, Weir
Furnival, J. & T.: Indian Jar
Furnival, Thomas: Indian Jar
Furnival, Thomas & Sons: Ceylon
Furnivals: Bouquet, Carnation, Versailles
Grimwade Bros.: Linnea, Venice
Grimwades Ltd.: Nelson
Grindley, W.H. & Co.: Alaska, Albany, Aldine, Argyle, Baltic, Beauty Roses, Blue Rose, Campion, Celtic, Clarence, Clifton, Denmark, Duchess, Florida, Girton, Glentine, The Hofburg, The Imperial, Janette, Keele, Le Pavot, Lorne, Marechal Noil, Marie, Marguerite, The Marquis, Melbourne, The Olympia, Osborne, Portman, Progress, The Regal, Rose, Shanghai, Somerset, Syrian, Waverly; see also Plate 378
H. Bros.: Petunia
Hancock, Sampson & Sons: Larch, Leicester, Welbeck
Heath, Joseph: Tonquin
Hollinshead & Kirkham: Davenport, Natal
Hughes, Thomas: Shapoo
Johnson Bros.: Andorra, Argyle, Astoria, Brooklyn, Claremont, Coral, Dorothy, Eclipse, Florida, Georgia, Holland, Jewel,

Mongolia, Normandy, Oxford, Peach, Persian, Richmond, Savoy, St. Louis, Sterling, Tulip, Turin
Johnson, Samuel, Ltd.: see Plate 347
Jones, Albert E.: Pekin
Jones, C. or G.: Wild Rose
Jones, George & Sons: Abbey
Keeling & Co.: Napier; see also Plate 358
L.A.: Oriental
Lockhart & Arthur: Anemone
Maddock, John & Sons: Belfort, Gem, Hamilton, Merian, Orchid, Roseville
Mayer, T.J. & J.: Arabesque, Formosa, Oregon
Meakin, Alfred: Cambridge, Devon, Kelvin, Messina
Meakin, J. & G.: Colonial, Geisha, Japan Pattern, Ormonde, Pagoda, Regina, Sol; see also Plates 326, 334, 350
Meigh, Charles: Hong Kong
Meir, John (I. or J.): Chen-Si
Minton: Delft; see also Plate 351
Minton & Boyle: Dagger Border
Myott, Son & Co.: Crumlin, Grosvenor, Rose
New Wharf Pottery Co.: Conway, Dunbarton, Gladys, Killarney, Knox, Lancaster, Louis, Monarch, Paris, Plymouth, Seville, Sterling, Trent, Waldorf
Phillips, George: Lobelia
Podmore, Walker & Co.: Manilla, The Temple
Poutney & Co.: Mandarin
Rathbone, T. & Co.: Japan, Princess, Trentham
Ridgway & Morley: Cashmere
Ridgway, William: Penang
Ridgways: Dundee, Ebor, Gainsborough, Josephine, Lonsdale, Lugano, Oriental, Osborne, Paqueminot, Rose, Roxbury, Saskia, Sefton, Turkey, Verona
R. & M. Co.: Auld Lang Syn, Theodore Roosevelt
Royal Staffordshire Pottery: see Arthur Wilkinson
Samuel Ford & Co.: Lonsdale
Stanley Pottery Co.: Touraine
Till, T. & Sons: Cecil
Upper Hanley Pottery Co.: Dahlia, Geisha, Venice
W in diamond shape: Lahore
W. & B.: Doric
Walley, Edward: see Plate 393
Weatherby, J.H. & Sons: Belmont
Wedgwood & Co.: Corinthia, Cows
Wedgwood, J.: see John Wedge Wood
Wedgwood, Josiah: Chinese, Hollyhock, Ivanhoe; see also Plates 335, 360
Wilkinson, Arthur J.: Arcadia, Jenny Lind, Yeddo
Wiltshaw & Robinson: Petunia; see also Plates 331, 352, 366, 374
Winkle, F. & Co.: Rudyard, Togo
Wood, John Wedge: Chapoo, Peruvian
Wood & Sons: Brunswick, Duchess, Lakewood, Madras, Seville, Syndey, Victoria

17

Non-English Manufacturers

Austria: Schmidt & Co., Plate 397
France: Jean Pouyat, Plate 398; Utzchneider & Co., Plate 399
Germany: F.A. Mehlem, Plate 400; Villeroy & Boch, Plates 401, 404; Unidentified, Plates 402, 403
Holland: Petrus Regout, Plates 405, 406; Societie Ceramique, Plate 407
Japan: TA in clover shape, Plate 408
Portugal: Gilman & Company, Plate 409

Prussia: Schlegelmilch, Plate 412; Unidentified, Plates 410, 411
United States: Burgess & Campbell, Plate 413; The Colonial Company, Plate 414; The French China Company, Plates 415-419; J. & E. Mayer, Plate 420; Mellor & Co., Plate 421; Mercer Pottery Co., Plate 422; Sebring Pottery, Plate 423; Warwick China Company, Plates 424-427; Wheeling Pottery Co., Plates 428-433

Non-English Patterns

Argyle, Plate 420
Balmoral, Plate 413
Delph, Plate 423
Fasan, Plate 404

Honc, Plate 405
Jardiniere, Plate 401
La Belle, Plates 428-433
La Francaise, Plates 415-419

Libertas, Plates 410, 411
Meissen, Plate 400
Royal Blue, Plate 413
U.S.S. Maine, Plate 416

U.S.S. Brooklyn, Plate 415
Vernon, Plate 421
Warwick, Plates 424-426

Manufacturers' Initials (English, unless noted)

B.B.--Minton (Best Body)
B. & C.--Burgess & Campbell, United States
B. & L.--Burgess & Leigh
B-W.M. & Co.--Brown-Westhead, Moore & Co.
D.--Thomas Dimmock
E.B. & J.E.L.--Bourne & Leigh
F.A.M. (monogram)--F.A. Mehlem, Germany
F. & Sons--Ford & Sons
F.W. & Co.--F. Winkle & Co.
G.B. (monogram in star shape), Grimwade Bros.
J. & E.--Mayer, United States
J.H.--Joseph Heath
J.H.W. & Sons--J.H. Weatherby
J.P. over L.--Jean Pouyat, Limoges, France
J. & T.F.Co.--Jacob and Thomas Furnival
K. & Co.--Keeling & Co.
K. & G.--Keller and Guerin, Luneville, France

L. & A.--Lockhart and Arthur
M. & B.--Minton & Boyle
N.W.P.--New Wharf Pottery
P.W. & Co.--Podmore, Walker, and Co.
R. & M. (under coat of arms)--Ridgway & Morley
S.A. & Co.--Samuel Alcock
S.F. & Co.--Samuel Ford
S.H. & Sons--Samuel Hancock & Sons
T.F. & Co.--Thomas Fell or Thomas Furnival
T.R. & Co. (under Swan mark)--Thomas Rathbone
V. & B.--Villeroy and Boch, Germany
W.E.C. (in script monogram in circle with crown)--W. & E. Corn
W.P.--Wheeling Pottery, United States
W.R.--William Ridgway
W. & R.--Wiltshaw & Robinson

Ambiguous Marks

Albion Pottery--Bourne & Leigh, England
Bisto--Bishop & Stonier, England
Colonial Potteries--F. Winkle, England
Kaolin Ware--Thomas Dimmock, England
Improved Stone China impressed in rectangular shaped mark--Charles Meigh, England
La Belle China--Wheeling Pottery, United States
La Francaise--The French China Co., United States
Libertas--see Mark 157
Middleport Pottery--Burgess & Leigh, England
New Stone, impressed mark--Minton, England

Opaque de Sarreguemines--Utzchneider & Co., France
Oriental Stone, impressed mark--J. & G. Alcock, England
Pearl, impressed mark--Josiah Wedgwood, England
Royal Semi-Porcelain--see Mark 31
Royal Staffordshire Pottery--Arthur J. Wilkinson, England
The Sebring--Sebring Pottery, United States
Wedgwood & Co.--Unicorn and Pinnox Works, England (not Josiah Wedgwood, England)
Wedgwood, J.--John Wedge Wood, England (not Josiah Wedgwood, England)

Objects (Other than Plates)

Bacon Platter--Plates 37, 233, 281

Berry Bowl or Fruit Dish--Plates 95, 148, 221, 225, 237, 241, 255, 308, 399, 419

Biscuit Jar--Plates 232, 246, 323, 324

Bone Dish--Plates 19, 63, 92, 239, 282, 325

Bowl & Pitcher Set--Plates 3, 198, 272, 319, 374-376

Bowl to Wash Set--Plates 65, 91, 423

Bread & Butter Plates--Plates 5, 41, 106, 169, 182, 184, 254, 398, 429

Butter Dish--Plates 145, 249, 258, 326

Butter Pat--Plates 129, 137, 286, 327, 328, 422

Cake Plate--Plates 149, 204, 329, 330, 391

Cake Stand--Plate 315

Chamber Pot--Plates 105, 197, 293, 318, 377, 378

Charger--Plate 102

Cheese Dish--Plates 331, 332

Chocolate Pot--Plates 309, 333

Coffee Pot--Plate 334

Creamer--Plates 4, 36, 40, 93, 94, 212, 247, 285, 313, 316

Cream & Sugar Set--Plates 248, 284

Cup (Cup & Saucer)--Plates 1, 11, 22, 39, 47, 57, 76, 89, 109, 155, 171, 202, 206-208, 215, 218, 261, 263, 271, 336-342, 387, 395, 401, 409

Cuspidor--Plate 35

Egg Holder--Plate 304

Foot Bath--Plate 118

Gravy Boat--Plates 15, 34, 81, 151, 192, 310, 311, 343

Handleless Cup--Plates 58, 140, 179, 335, 394

Hot Water Dish--Plate 174

Hot Water Jug--Plate 231

Jam Dish--Plate 51

Jardiniere--Plate 243

Ladle--Plate 153

Molasses Pitcher--Plate 425

Mustache Cup--Plate 48

Oyster Plate--Plate 84

Pitcher--Plates 62, 71, 79, 110, 160, 175, 209, 252, 288, 344-353, 389, 390, 417, 418, 420, 431

Platter--Plates 9, 12, 13, 23, 42, 61, 77, 78, 101, 112, 114, 126, 130, 156, 157, 173, 187, 194, 203, 211, 214, 257, 267, 277, 291, 297, 303, 322

Portrait or Commemorative Pieces--Plates 57, 111, 113, 136, 185, 397, 415, 416

Punch Bowl--Plates 67, 296

Relish Dish--Plates 14, 45, 362, 363, 396, 424

Sauce Tureen--Plates 213, 236

Soap Dish--Plates 197, 252, 272, 375, 381

Shaving Mug--Plates 252, 386, 388

Shredded Wheat Dish--Plate 2

Spoonholder--Plate 205

Sugar Bowl--Plates 29, 75, 104, 123, 253, 364

Soup Bowl--Plates 8, 44, 46, 70, 100, 103, 117, 128, 191, 240, 321, 384, 407, 413

Soup Plate--Plates 30, 49, 53, 74, 85, 120, 159, 176, 178, 181, 200, 217, 219, 260, 283, 295

Tea Pot--Plates 365, 366

Toast Rack--Plate 367

Toothbrush Holder--Plates 43, 135, 197, 272, 375, 379-382

Tray--Plates 16, 17, 32, 163, 427

Trinket Box--Plate 412

Trivet--Plates 352, 366

Tureen--Plates 6, 56, 153, 368, 369

Vase--Plates 64, 370, 371

Vegetable or Fruit Bowl (open or covered)--Plates 18, 24, 31, 50, 68, 72, 82, 98, 107, 108, 121, 124, 133, 141, 147, 164, 165, 167, 188, 195, 196, 216, 222, 234, 235, 238, 256, 266, 268, 280, 289, 290, 298, 299, 306, 307, 312, 372, 400, 414, 421, 430, 432, 433

Waste Bowl--Plates 69, 88, 166, 317, 383, 385

Waste Jar--Plate 273

English Marks

2. William Adams & Sons, circa
1819-1864.

1. William Adams & Sons, circa
1819-1864.

3. William Adams & Co., England, after
1891.

4. William Adams & Co., England, after
1891.

5. William Adams & Co., England, after
1891.

6. William Adams & Co., England, after
1891.

7. William Adams & Co., England, after
1891.

8. William Adams & Co., Tunstall,
England, after 1896.

9. William Adams & Co., Tunstall,
England, after 1896.

10. William and Thomas Adams, circa 1866-1892.

11. Henry Alcock & Co., England, circa 1891-1900.

12. John and George Alcock, Cobridge, circa 1839-1846.

13. John and George Alcock, impressed initials with "Oriental Stone," circa 1839-1846.

14. Samuel Alcock & Co., initials, circa 1830-1859.

15. Charles Allerton & Sons, England, after 1891 and probably before 1912.

16. Allertons, mark in banner under crown, England, circa 1903-1912.

17. Ashworth, G.L., impressed crown with name, circa 1862-1880.

18. Ashworth, G.L. & Bros., crown with A. Bros. and banner underneath, circa 1862-1890.

19. Ashworth, G.L. & Bros., lion over scroll with G.L.A. Bros. and pattern name, circa 1862-1890.

20. Bishop & Stonier, "Bisto," circa 1891-1936.

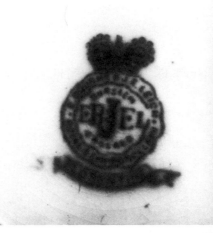

21. Bourne & Leigh, "E. Bourne and J.E Leigh, Burslem, England" plus initials circa 1892-1939.

22. Bourne & Leigh, "Albion Pottery," plus initials, circa 1912-1941.

23. Brown-Westhead, Moore & Co., Cauldon, England, circa 1895-1904.

24. Burgess & Leigh, Middleport Pottery with initials, after 1889 to 1919.

25. Burgess & Leigh, Middleport Pottery, England, circa 1891-1919.

26. Burgess & Leigh, Burslem, England, circa 1906-1912.

27. Burgess & Leigh, Middleport Pottery Burslem, England, circa 1906-1912.

28. Burgess & Leigh, initials with England, circa 1891-1919.

29. Cauldon, England, circa 1905-1920.

30. E. Challinor, circa 1842-1867.

31. Possibly Edward Clark, circa 1877-1887.

32. Clementson & Young, circa 1845-1847.

33. Alfred Colley, Ltd, Tunstall, England, circa 1909-1914.

34. W. & E. Corn, "Porcelain Royal," circa 1900-1904.

35. W. & E. Corn, monogram with "Porcelain Royale Art Ware, England," circa 1900-1904.

36. W. & E. Corn, England, circa 1900-1904.

37. Davenport, impressed anchor mark, circa early 1800's to circa 1860 for this type of mark. The one shown here is for 1844 with an impressed "4" on either side of the anchor.

38. Dean, S.W. & Co., circa 1904-1910.

39. Dimmock, Thomas, circa 1828-1859.

40. Doulton & Co., circa 1882-1890.

41. Doulton & Co., England, circa 1891-1902.

42. Doulton & Co., Burslem, England, circa 1891-1902.

43. Doulton & Co., Burslem, England, circa 1891-1902.

44. Doulton & Co., Royal Doulton, England, circa 1902-1930.

45. Doulton & Co., Royal Doulton, Burslem, England, circa 1902-1930.

46. Doulton & Co., Made in England, after 1930.

47. Doulton & Co., Royal Doulton, Made in England, after 1930.

48. E.W. particular company not identified.

49. T. Edwards, particular company not identified, may be Thomas Edwards, circa 1839-41.

50. T. Fell & Co., circa 1830-1890, printed initials with impressed "Real Iron Stone."

51. Ford & Sons, circa 1893-1907.

52. Ford & Sons, Ltd., circa 1908-1930.

53. Jacob & Thomas Furnival, circa 1843, printed initials.

54. Thomas Furnival & Co. circa 1844-1846, printed initials.

55. Furnival & Sons, printed in upper part of mark, circa 1871-1890.

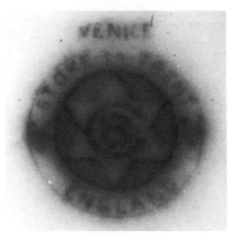

56. Grimwade Bros., initials printed, circa 1886-1900.

57. Grimwades, after 1903, profile of a lady in center of mark.

58. Grimwades, circa 1906 and after.

59. W.H. Grindley & Co., England, circa 1891-1914.

60. W.H. Grindley & Co., England, circa 1891-1914.

61. W.H. Grindley & Co., England, circa 1914-1925.

62. H. Bros., Tunstall, England, after 1891, no company identified.

63. Sampson Hancock & Sons, Stoke-on-Trent, England, circa 1906-1912.

64. Sampson Hancock & Sons, England, initials, circa 1906-1912.

65. Sampson Hancock & Sons, England, initials, circa 1906-1912.

66. J. Heath, printed initials and impressed "J. Heath," probably Joseph Heath, circa 1845-1853 although Godden notes that there were other J. Heaths working in Staffordshire at the same time.

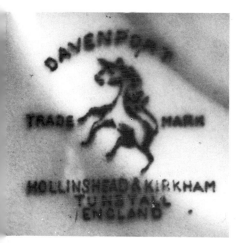

67. Hollinshead & Kirkham, Tunstall, England, circa 1900-1924.

68. Thomas Hughes, Longport, England, circa 1860-1890.

69. Thomas Hughes & Son, Ltd., England, circa 1910-1930.

70. Johnson Bros., England, circa 1900 and after.

71. Johnson Bros., England, circa 1900 and after.

72. Johnson Bros., England, circa 1900 and after.

73. Johnson Bros., England, circa 1913 and after.

74. Samuel Johnson, Ltd., Britannia Pottery, circa 1913-1931.

75. G. (or C.) Jones, England, may be George Jones.

76. George Jones & Sons, circa 1864-1907.

77. Keeling & Co., circa 1886-1891, initials.

78. Keeling & Co. Ltd., circa 1912-1936

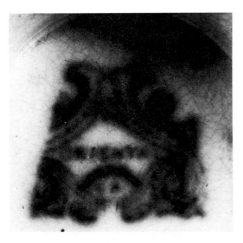

79. L.A., company not identified.

80. Lockhart and Arthur, initials, circa 1855-1864.

81. John Maddock, impressed mark with name and castle and "Ironstone China," circa 1842-1855.

82. John Maddock, printed oriental style mark accompanying impressed mark (preceding), circa 1842-1855.

83. John Maddock and Sons, England, circa 1880-1896.

84. T.J. & J. Mayer, Longport, initials, circa 1843 to probably mid 1850's.

85. T.J. & J. Mayer, initials, circa 1843 to mid 1850's.

86. Alfred Meakin, Ltd., circa 1897-1930.

87. Alfred Meakin, Ltd., circa 1907-1930.

88. J. & G. Meakin, Hanley, England, after 1890.

89. J. & G. Meakin, Hanley, England, circa 1890 and after.

90. J. & G. Meakin, Hanley, England (written in mark under crown), circa 1912 and after.

91. J. & G. Meakin, England, circa 1912 and after.

92. Charles Meigh or Charles Meigh & Son, impressed mark "Improved Stone China" in rectangle, circa 1835-1861.

93. John Meir, initials which may be "I" or "J"M., circa 1812-1836.

94. Minton & Boyle, initials, circa 1836-1841; Impressed "B.B." and "New Stone."

95. Mintons, impressed name and registry mark, this type of mark is circa 1873-1891.

96. Myott, Son & Co., initials under crown, circa 1900 and after.

97. Myott, Son & Co., printed "Imperial Semi Porcelain" over crown and name underneath, circa 1907 and after.

98. New Wharf Pottery Co., circa 1890-1894.

99. New Wharf Pottery Co., circa 1890-1894.

100. New Wharf Pottery Co., circa 1890-1894.

101. George Phillips, circa 1834-1848 for type of mark.

102. Podmore, Walker & Co., initials in oriental style mark, "P.W. & Co." with "Ironstone" underneath, circa 1834-1859.

103. Podmore, Walker & Co., "Pearl Stone Ware" written in outer circle of mark with pattern name inside and "Wedgwood" in ribbon underneath, circa 1849-1859.

104. Poutney & Co. Ltd., printed name in triangle shaped mark with "Bristol" and name of pattern, crossed swords with "1750" inside triangle, circa 1900 and after.

105. T. Rathbone & Co., initials, circa 1912-1923.

106. Ridgway & Morley, coat of arms with initials "R & M" underneath, circa 1842-1844.

107. William Ridgway, initials, circa 1830-1834.

108. Ridgways, Beehive and Urn mark, England, after 1891 to circa 1920.

109. Ridgways, circa 1905-1920.

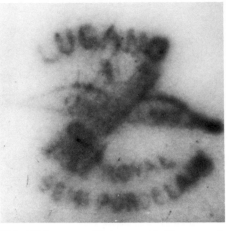

110. Ridgways, Quiver and Bow mark with "Ridgways" on quiver and "England" inside bow and "Royal Semi Porcelain" underneath, circa 1912-1920. This mark without England may have "Stoke-on-Trent" which dates from 1880.

111. R. & M. Co., company not identified

112. Samuel Ford & Co. B. Ltd., Lincoln Pottery, England, 1898-1939.

113. Stanley Pottery Co., England, circa 1928-1931.

114. Thomas Till & Sons, circa 1891-1928

115. Upper Hanley Pottery, England, printed in mark under crown, circa 1895-1900.

116. W in diamond shape, England, company not identified, after 1891.

117. W in diamond shape with Englan above mark, company not identified, aft 1891.

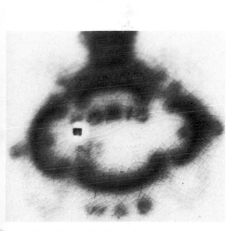

118. W. & B., initials under crown and ornate mark containing pattern name, company not identified.

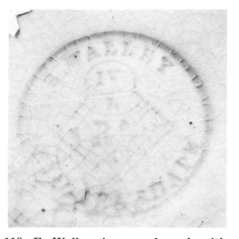

119. E. Walley, impressed mark with name and registry mark in circle, wording in bottom half of mark illegible, circa 1845-1856.

120. J.H. Weatherby & Sons, initials, circa 1892 and after.

121. Wedgwood & Co., England, circa 1890-1900.

122. Wedgwood & Co., Ltd., England, circa 1908 and after.

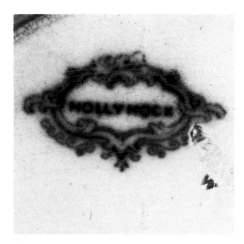

123. Josiah Wedgwood, impressed name with upper case letters and "PEARL" impressed, circa 1840-1868.

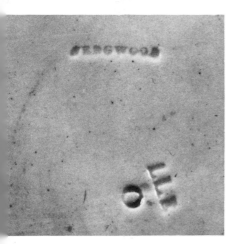

124. Josiah Wedgwood, impressed WEDGWOOD" in upper case letters with impressed letters of "LLE" indicating date of 1876.

125. Arthur J. Wilkinson, "Royal Staffordshire Pottery" in ribbon beneath lion and crown, Burslem, England, circa 1907.

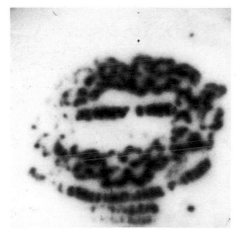

126. Arthur J. Wilkinson, "Royal Staffordshire Pottery, Burslem, England" printed under ornate floral mark containing pattern name, circa early 1900's.

127. Wiltshaw & Robinson, initials, circa 1894-1957.

128. F. Winkle & Co., initials, circa 1890-1910.

129. F. Winkle & Co., initials with "Colonial Pottery, Stoke, England," circa 1890-1925.

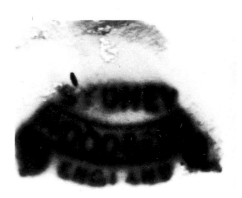

130. John Wedge Wood, printed "J. Wedgwood" on ribbon at bottom of mark, circa 1841-1860.

131. Wood & Son, England, circa 1891-1907.

132. Wood & Son, England, circa 1891-1907.

133. Divided rectangular printed mark with "Indian" pattern name, company not identified.

134. Ornate scroll and floral mark, company not identified, "Chinese Pagoda" pattern.

135. Pattern name "Lahore" with England, after 1891, company not identified.

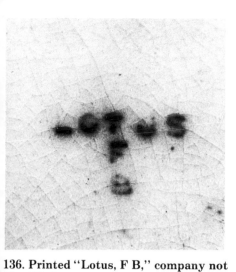

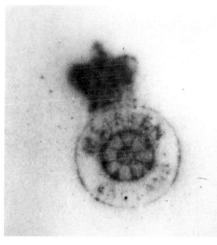

136. Printed "Lotus, F B," company not identified.

137. Crown and circle mark with pattern name "Meissen" and "England," after 1891, company not identified.

138. Crown mark with pattern name "Orleans" and "Stoneware" beneath, company not identified.

139. Printed mark with pattern name "Sobraon," company not identified.

140. Printed mark with pattern name "Simlay," company not identified.

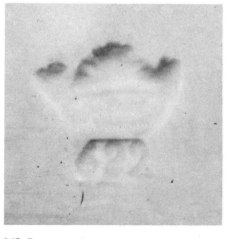

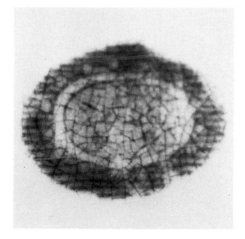

141. Crown and circle mark with lion and pattern name "Watteau," and "Staffordshire, England," after 1891, company not identified.

142. Impressed crown mark, company not identified.

143. Printed mark of oval shape, composed of inner circle and horizontal lines, company not identified.

Non-English Marks

144. Jean Pouyat, Limoges, France, initials, circa 1891-1914.

145. Keller and Guerin, Luneville, France, after 1891.

146. Utzchneider & Co., Sarreguemines, France, circa 19th century.

147. W in diamond shape with "Quebec" as pattern name and "Germany," company not identified, after 1891.

148. Crown and shield mark, "Made in Germany," possibly Utzchneider & Co., 20th century mark.

149. F.A. Mehlem, Germany, impressed mark, 19th century.

150. F.A. Mehlem, Germany, printed mark, initials, Germany, after 1891.

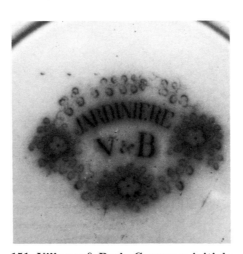

151. Villeroy & Boch, Germany, initials, mid 19th century.

152. Villeroy & Boch, Germany, initials, mid 19th century.

153. Petrus Regout, Maastricht, Holland, 20th century mark.

154. Societie Ceramique, Maastricht, Holland, 20th century mark.

155. T.A., Made in Japan, company not identified, 20th century mark.

156. Gilman & Company, Portugal, after 1891, company not identified.

157. Libertas, "Prussia," company not identified.

158. Burgess & Campbell, Trenton, New Jersey, company established in 1879.

159. Burgess & Campbell, Trenton, New Jersey, after 1879.

160. Burgess & Campbell, Trenton, New Jersey, impressed mark with names and lion in circle.

161. The Colonial Co., company not identified.

162. The French China Co., Sebring, Ohio, circa 1900-1916.

163. The French China Co., Sebring, Ohio, circa 1900-1916.

164. J. & E. Mayer, Beaver Falls, Pennsylvania, company established in 1881.

165. Mellor & Co., Trenton, New Jersey, established circa 1894.

166. Mercer Pottery Co., Trenton, New Jersey, established in 1868.

167. Wheeling Pottery Co., Wheeling, West Virginia, after 1893.

168. Wheeling Pottery Co., Wheeling, West Virginia, after 1893.

English Patterns

PLATE 1. ABBEY, George Jones, Mark 76. Cup, 3″h; Saucer, 6″d.

PLATE 2. ABBEY, George Jones, Mark 76. Marked "Shredded Wheat Dish," over pattern mark, 6¼″l, 5″w.

PLATE 3. ABBEY, George Jones, Mark 76. Bowl and Pitcher Set.

PLATE 4. ALASKA, W.H. Grindley, Mark 59. Creamer, 5¼″h.

PLATE 5. ALBANY, W.G. Grindley, Mark 60. Bread & Butter Plate, 6½″d.

PLATE 6. ALDINE, W.H. Grindley, Mark 59. Footed Tureen, 12″l, 8″h.

PLATE 7. AMOY, Davenport, Mark 37. Plate, 9″d.

PLATE 8. ANDORRA, Johnson Bros., Mark 73. Soup Bowl, 7½″d.

PLATE 9. ANEMONE, Lockhart & Arthur, Mark 80. Plater, 16″l, 13″w.

PLATE 10. ARABESQUE, T.J. & J. Mayer, Mark 84. Plate, 10″d.

PLATE 11. ARCADIA, Arthur J. Wilkinson, Mark 125. Cup, 2¼″h, 3¼″d; Saucer, 5½″d.

PLATE 12. ARGYLE, W.H. Grindley, Mark 60. Platter 13″l, 9″w.

PLATE 13. ARGYLE, W.H. Grindley, Marks 59 & 60. Platter, 12″l, 8″w.

PLATE 14. ARGYLE, W.H. Grindley, Mark 59. Relish 8½″l.

PLATE 15. ARGYLE, W.H. Grindley, Mark 59. Gravy Boat, scalloped footed base, 3½"h, 8"l.

PLATE 16. ARGYLE, Ford & Sons, Mark 51. Tray, 10¼"l, 8"w.

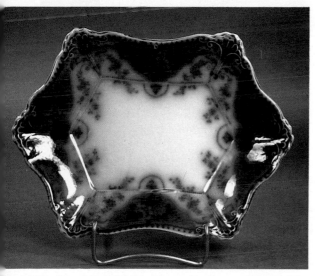

PLATE 17. ARGYLE, Ford & Sons, Mark 51. Tray, six sided, 9"l, 6¼"w.

PLATE 18. ARGYLE. Piece is unmarked but pattern is like Ford & Son's "Argyle." Covered Bowl, six sided, 7"h, 12¼"l, 8"w.

PLATE 19. ARGYLE, Johnson Bros., Mark 73. Bone Dish, 6¼″l.

PLATE 20. ASIATIC PHEASANTS, W. & T. Adams, Mark 10. Plate, 11″d.

PLATE 21. ASTORIA, Johnson Bros., Mark 70. Plate, 10¼"d.

PLATE 22. AULD LANG SYN, R. & M. Co., Mark 111. Cup, 3½"h, 5½"d.

PLATE 23. AYR, W. & E. Corn, Mark 36. Platter, 10¼"l, ½"w.

PLATE 24. AYR, W. & E. Corn, Mark 36. Vegetable Bowl, 4"h, 8"d.

PLATE 25. BALTIC, W.H. Grindley, Mark 59. Plate, 10″d.

PLATE 26. BEAUTY ROSES, W.H. Grindley, Mark 6I Plate, 9″d.

PLATE 27. BELFORT, John Maddock & Sons, Mark 83. Plate, 8½″d.

PLATE 28. BELMONT, J.H. Weatherby & Sons, Mar 120. Plate, 9″d.

PLATE 29. BERLIN GROUPS, W. Adams & Sons, Mark 2. Covered Sugar, 8 sided, set includes
Coffee Pot and Creamer not shown.

PLATE 30. BEVERLY, Doulton, Mark 43. Soup Plate, 10½″d.

PLATE 31. BLOSSOM, S.W. Dean, Mark 38. Vegetabl Bowl, 10″d.

PLATE 32. "Blue Rose," p. 89, Williams' Book I. W.H. Grindley, Mark 60. Oval Tray, 10″l.

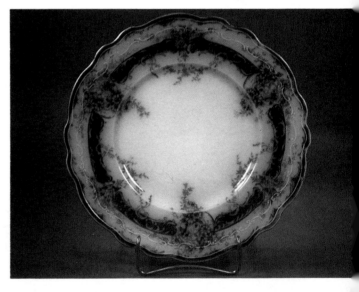

PLATE 33. BOUQUET, Henry Alcock, Mark 11. Plat 9″d.

PLATE 34. BOUQUET, Henry Alcock, Mark 11. Gravy Boat, 4"h, 9"l.

PLATE 35. BOUQUET, Marked "Furnivals, Ltd.," Mark not shown, after 1913. Cuspidor, 2½"h, 8"d.

PLATE 36. BREADLEBANE, Brown-Westhead, Moore, & Co., Mark 23. Creamer, 4½"h.

49

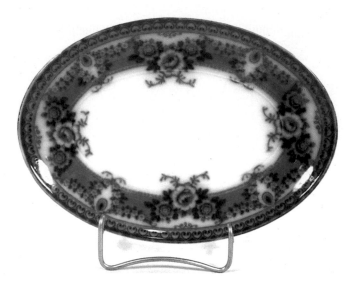

PLATE 37. BRISTOL, Ford & Sons, Mark 52. Bacon Platter, 9″l.

PLATE 38. BROOKLYN, Johnson Bros., Mark 70. Plate, 8½″d.

PLATE 39. BROOKLYN, Johnson Bros., Mark 70. Cup, 2″h, 4″d; Saucer, 6″d.

PLATE 40. BROOKLYN, Johnson Bros., Mark 70. Creamer, 5½″h.

PLATE 41. BRUNSWICK, Wood & Son, Mark 131. Bread & Butter Plate, 7″d.

PLATE 42. BURLEIGH, Burgess & Leigh, Mark 27. Platter, 16″l.

PLATE 43. BUTTERCUP, Doulton, Mark 43. Toothbrush Holder, 6″h.

PLATE 44. CABUL, T. Edwards, Mark 49. Bowl, 8¼″d.

PLATE 45. CAMBRIDGE, A. Meakin, Mark 86. Relish, 8½″l, 5¼″w.

PLATE 46. CAMBRIDGE, A. Meakin, Mark 86. This piece did not have the pattern name with the manufacturer's mark. Soup Bowl, 7½″d.

PLATE 48. CAMPION, W.H. Grindley, Mark 59. Mustache Cup, 3½″h.

PLATE 47. CAMBRIDGE, A. Meakin, Mark 86. Cup, 3″h, 3″d; Saucer, 6″d.

PLATE 49. CANDIA, Cauldon, Mark 29 and also "Cauldon" impressed. Soup Plate, 9″d.

PLATE 50. CARNATION, Marked "Furnivals," mark not shown, circa 1890-1895. Vegetable Bowl, 3½″h, 9½″d.

PLATE 51. CASHMERE, Ridgway & Morley, Mark 106.
Jam Dish, 3½"h, underplate, 7"d, figural lion heads serve
as handles.

PLATE 52. CECIL, Till & Sons, Mark 114. Plate, 9½"d.

PLATE 53. CELESTE, Burgess & Leigh, Mark 28. Soup
Plate, 10½"d, polychromed.

PLATE 54. CELTIC, W.H. Grindley, Mark 60. Plate, 9"d.

PLATE 55. CEYLON, T. Furnival & Sons, Mark 55. Underplate to Covered Tureen, 15½″l, 10″d.

PLATE 56. CEYLON. Matching Tureen to Underplate in Plate 55, 12″h, 15″l.

PLATE 57. CHAIN OF STATES. Popular name for pattern. Pieces have no manufacturer's mark, but say, "Made in England for Oran M. Shaw, Portsmouth, New Hampshire," on 9″ Plate, and "Made in England for Daniel Low & Co., Salem, Mass," on 6″ Saucer. Cup is 2½″h.

PLATE 58. CHAPOO, John Wedge Wood, Mark 130. Handleless Cup, 3″h; Saucer, 6″d.

PLATE 59. CHEN SI, J.M. Mier, Mark 3. Plate 10½″d.

55

PLATE 60. CHINESE, Bourne & Leigh, Mark 22. Plate, 9½″d.

PLATE 61. CHINESE, Thomas Dimmock, Mark 39. Platter, 17½″l, 14″w.

PLATE 63. CHINESE, Josiah Wedgwood, Mark 124 (Impressed Name). Turkey Bone Dish, 6½″l, 4″w, one of a set of six.

PLATE 62. CHINESE, Thomas Dimmock, Mark 39. Pitcher, 9″h.

PLATE 64. CHINESE, Josiah Wedgwood, Printed Mark, "Wedgwood, Etruria," Mark not shown, Vase, 12″h.

PLATE 65. CHINESE PAGODA, Mark 134, Bowl to Wash Set, 7″h, 15½″d.

PLATE 66. CHINESE PLANT, E.W., Mark 48. Plate, 9¼″d.

PLATE 67. "Chusan," p. 38, Williams' Book II. Unmarked. Punch Bowl, 7"h, 12" across.

PLATE 68. CIRCASSIA, J. & G. Alcock, Mark 12. Covered Bowl, 8"h, 15"d., pedestal base.

PLATE 69. CLAREMONT, Johnson Bros., Mark 70.
Waste Bowl, 3"h.

PLATE 70. CLARENCE, W.H. Grindley, Mark 59. Sou
Bowl, 7½"d.

PLATE 72. COLONIAL, J. & G. Meakin, Mark 89.
Covered Vegetable, 7"h, 10"d.

PLATE 71. CLIFTON, W.H. Grindley, Mark
60. Pitcher, 8½"h.

PLATE 73. CONWAY, New Wharf Pottery, Mark 98.
late, 9″d.

PLATE 74. CORAL, Johnson Bros., Mark 73. Soup Plate,
9″d.

LATE 75. CORAL, Johnson Bros., Mark 73.
overed Sugar, 5½″h.

PLATE 76. CORINTHIA, Wedgwood & Co., Mark 121. Cup,
2½″h; Saucer, 6″d.

PLATE 77. COUNTRY SCENES, Marked "England." Platter, 11″l.

PLATE 78. COWS, Wedgwood & Co., Mark 122. Platter, 17″l, 13½″w.

PLATE 79. CRUMLIN, Myott's, Mark 96.
Pitcher, 10"h.

PLATE 80. CRUMLIN, Moytt's, Mark 96. Plate, 9"d.

PLATE 81. DAGGER BORDER, Minton & Boyle, Mark 94.
Gravy Boat, 6"l.

PLATE 82. "Dahlia," p. 96, Williams' Book I. Upper Hanley Pottery, Mark 115. Bowl, 11"d.

PLATE 83. DAVENPORT, Hollinshead & Kirkham, Mark
. Plate, 6½"sq.

PLATE 84. DELFT, Minton, Mark 95. Oyster plate, 9"d.

PLATE 85. DENMARK, W.H. Grindley, Mark 59. Soup Plate, 10″d.

PLATE 86. DEVON, A. Meakin, Mark 87. Platter, 14″l, 10″w

PLATE 87. DORIC, W. & B., Mark 118. Plate, 9½″d.

PLATE 88. DOROTHY, W. & E. Corn, Mark 34. Wast Bowl, 3½″h, 6″d.

PLATE 89. DOROTHY, W. & E. Corn, Mark 34. Cup, 2½″h, Saucer, 5½″d.

PLATE 90. DUCHESS, W. H. Grindley, Mark 59. Plat 10″d.

PLATE 91. DUCHESS, Wood & Son, Mark 131. Bowl to Wash Set, 17¼"d.

PLATE 92. DUNBARTON, New Wharf Pottery, Mark 98. Bone Dish, 6½"l, 3"w.

PLATE 93. DUNDEE, Ridgways, Mark 110. Creamer, ½"h.

PLATE 94. EBOR, Ridgways, Mark 110. Creamer, 5¼"h.

PLATE 95. ECLIPSE, Johnson Bros., Mark 70. Berry Bowl, 5¼"d.

PLATE 96. EXCELSIOR, T. Fell, Mark 50. Plate, 9"d.

PLATE 97. FAIRY VILLAS, W. Adams and Co., Mark 5. This is one version of the pattern by Adams. See Plate 98 for another version. Plate, 10″d.

PLATE 98. FAIRY VILLAS, W. Adams and Co., Mark 6. Bowl, 10″d.

PLATE 99. FLANNEL DAISY, W. & E. Corn, Mark 36. Plate, 9″d.

PLATE 100. FLORENTINE, Bourne & Leigh, Mark 21 Soup Bowl, 8½″d.

PLATE 101. FLORIDA, Johnson Bros., Mark 70. Platter, six sided, 15″l, 10″w.

PLATE 102. FLORIDA, W.H. Grindley, Mark 60. Charger, 15″d.

PLATE 103. FORMOSA, T.J. & J. Mayer, Mark 85. Bowl, 8½"d.

PLATE 104. GAINSBOROUGH, Ridgways, Mark 10 Covered Sugar, 6"h.

PLATE 105. GARLAND, W. Adams & Co., Mark 3. Chamber Pot, 5¼"h, 9"d.

PLATE 106. GEISHA, Ford & Sons, Mark 52. Bread & Butter Plate, 7"d.

PLATE 107. GEISHA, Upper Hanley Pottery, Mark 115. Bowl, 10"d.

PLATE 108. GEISHA, J. & G. Meakin, Mark 88. Oval Vegetable Bowl, 9"l.

PLATE 109. GEM, John Maddock & Sons, Mark 83 (with Ltd.," circa 1896 and after). Cup, 2½"h; Saucer, 6"d.

PLATE 110. GENEVA, Doulton, Mark 45. Pitcher, 6"h.

PLATE 111. GEORGE WASHINGTON, Doulton, Mark 44. Plate, 10¼"d.

PLATE 112. GEORGIA, Johnson Bros., Mark 73. Platter, 10"c

PLATE 113. GIBSON GIRL, Royal Doulton, Mark 47. Plate, 10½"d, one of a set. "She finds that exercise does not improve her spirits."

PLATE 114. GIRTON, W.H. Grindley, Marks 59 & 60. Platter, 16¼"l.

PLATE 115. GLADYS, New Wharf Pottery, Mark 98. Plate, 9½"d.

PLATE 116. GLENTINE, W.H. Grindley, Mark 61. Plat 10¼"d.

PLATE 117. GLORIA, W. Adams &
Co., Mark 8. Soup Bowl, 9½"d.

PLATE 118. GLORIE de DIJON,
Doulton, Mark 43. Foot Bath.

ATE 119. GROSVENOR, Myott,
& Co., Mark 97. Plate, 10"d.

PLATE 120. HAMILTON, John Maddock, Mark 83. Soup Plate, 9″d.

PLATE 121. "Hindustan," p. 27, Williams' Book I. Unmarked. Covered Vegetable Bowl, 8½″h, 11½″l.

PLATE 122. HIZEN, G.L. Ashworth, Mark 17 (without crown). Plate, 10½″d.

PLATE 123. THE HOFBURG, W.H. Grindley, Mark 5? Covered Sugar, 5½″h.

PLATE 124. HOLLAND, Johnson Bros., Mark 73. Covered Vegetable Bowl, 12½"l.

PLATE 125. HOLLYHOCK, Josiah Wedgwood, Mark 123. Plate, 10½"d.

PLATE 126. HOLLYHOCK, Josiah Wedgwood, Mark 123. Platter, 10"l, 7¼"w.

PLATE 127. HONG KONG, Charles Meigh, Mark 92. Plate, 8¼"d.

PLATE 128. HONG KONG, Charles Meigh, Mark 92. Pattern name was not on this piece. Bowl, 8"d.

PLATE 129. HONG KONG, Charles Meigh, Mark 92. Pattern name was not on this piece. Butter Pat, 4"d.

PLATE 130. THE IMPERIAL, W.H. Grindley, Mark 6? Platter, 12¼"l.

PLATE 131. INDIAN, Mark 133. Plate, 8¼"d.

PLATE 132. INDIAN JAR, J. & T. Furnival, Mark 5? Plate, 9"d.

PLATE 133. INDIAN JAR, T. Furnival & Co., Mark 54 with ''Real Iron Stone'' impressed. Octagonal shaped Bowl, 13″l, 10″w.

PLATE 134. IRIS, W. & E. Corn, Mark 35. Plate, 9″d.

PLATE 135. ITALIA, Burgess & Leigh, Mark 24. Toothbrush Holder, 6″h.

PLATE 136. IVANHOE, Josiah Wedgwood, Mark 124 with initials "AKB" impressed, circa 1899 and also printed mark "WEDGWOOD, ETRURIA, ENGLAND," Plate, 10¼"d. "Rebecca Repelling the Templar." One of a set.

PLATE 137. JANETTE, W.H. Grindley, Mark 59. Butter Pat, 3"d.

PLATE 138. JAPAN, T. Rathbone & Co., Mark 105. Plate, 10"d.

PLATE 139. JAPAN PATTERN, J. & G. Meakin, Mark 88. Plate, 10"d.

PLATE 140. JEDDO, W. Adams & Sons, Mark 1. Handleless cup, 3″h; Saucer, 6″d.

PLATE 141. JENNY LIND, Arthur J. Wilkinson, Mark 126. Vegetable Bowl, 3¼″h, 7½″d.

PLATE 142. JEWEL, Johnson Bros., Mark 71. Saucer, 6½″d.

PLATE 143. JOSEPHINE, Ridgways, Mark 110. Plate, 10″d.

PLATE 144. KEELE, W.H. Grindley, Mark 59. Plate, 10″d.

PLATE 145. KELVIN, Alfred Meakin, Mark 86. Underplate to Butter Dish, 7½″d.

PLATE 146. KHAN, Bishop & Stonier, Mark 20. Plate, 10½"d.

PLATE 147. KILLARNEY, New Wharf Pottery, Mark 98. Oval Vegetable Bowl, 10½"l.

PLATE 148. KNOX, New Wharf Pottery, Mark 98. Berry Bowl, 5"d.

PLATE 149. KREMLIN, Samuel Alcock, Mark 14. Cake Plate, 10¼"d.

PLATE 150. KYBER, W. Adams & Co., Mark 2. Plate, 9″d.

PLATE 151. KYBER, W. Adams & Co., Mark 2. Gravy Boat, 4″h, 7½″l.

PLATE 152. LAHORE, Mark 135. Note same pattern with Mark 117. Plate, 10½"d.

PLATE 153. LAKEWOOD, Wood & Son, Mark 131. Covered Tureen and Ladle.

PLATE 154. LANCASTER, Bishop & Stonier, Mark 20. Plate, 10¼"d.

PLATE 155. LANCASTER, New Wharf Pottery, Mark 98. Cup, 2½"h, Saucer; 5½"d.

PLATE 156. LARCH, Sampson Hancock & Sons, Mark 63. Platter, 12"l.

PLATE 157. LEICESTER, Sampson Hancock & Sons, Mark 65. Platter, 15"l, 12¼"w.

PLATE 158. LE PAVOT, W.H. Grindley, Mark 60. Plate 10"d.

PLATE 159. LINNEA, Grimwades, Mark 57. Soup Plate 10½"d.

PLATE 160. LOBELIA, George
Phillips, Mark 101. Milk Pitcher, 6″h.

PLATE 161. LOIS, New Wharf Pottery, Mark 99. Plate, 8″d.

PLATE 162. LOIS, New Wharf Pottery, Mark 98. Saucer, 6″d.

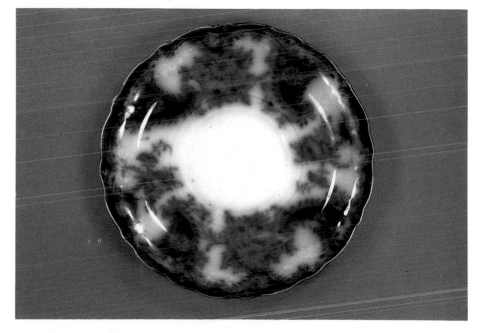

PLATE 163. LONSDALE, S. F. & Co., Mark 112. Tray, 11½″l, 9¼″w.

PLATE 164. LONSDALE, Ridgways, Mark 110. Covered Bowl, 7″h, 12½″l.

PLATE 165. LORNE, W.H. Grindley, Mark 59. Oval Vegetable Bowl, 9¼"l.

PLATE 166. LORNE, W.H. Grindley, Mark 59. Waste Bowl, 3¼"h, 6"d.

PLATE 167. LOTUS, Mark 136. Oval Vegetable Bowl, 10¼"l, 8"w.

PLATE 168. LUCANIA, Mark 31. Plate, 9"d.

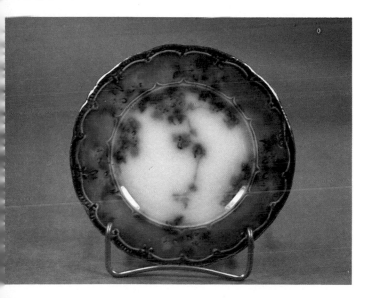

PLATE 169. LUGANO, Ridgways, Mark 110. Bread & Butter Plate, 5½"d.

PLATE 170. LUSITANIA, Alfred Colley, Ltd., Mark 33. Plate, 10"d.

PLATE 171. MABEL, Allertons, Mark 16. Cup, 2½"h, Saucer, 6"d.

PLATE 172. MADRAS, Doulton, Mark 42. Plate 10"d.

PLATE 173. MADRAS, Doulton, Mark 43. Platter, 16"l, 13"w.

PLATE 174. MADRAS, Doulton, Mark 47. No pattern name appears on this piece. Warming or Hot Water Tray 12"l, 8½"w.

PLATE 175. MADRAS, Royal Doulton, Mark 44. Pitcher, 8½"h, also one 7"h not shown.

PLATE 176. MADRAS. Wood & Son, Mark 131. Soup Plate, 9″d.

PLATE 177. MANDARIN, Pountney & Co., Ltd., Mark 104. Plate, 9″d.

PLATE 178. MANHATTAN, Henry Alcock, Mark 11. Soup Plate, 9″d.

PLATE 179. MANILLA, Podmore, Walker, & Co., Mark 102. Handleless Cup, 3½″h; Saucer, 6½″d.

PLATE 180. MANILLA, Podmore, Walker & Co., Mark 102. Plate, 9″d.

PLATE 181. MARECHAL NEIL, W.H. Grindley, Mark 59. Soup Plate, 8″d.

PLATE 182. MARIE, W.H. Grindley, Mark 59. Bread & Butter Plate, 7"d.

PLATE 183. MARGUERITE, W.H. Grindley, Mark 60. Plate, 8"d.

PLATE 184. THE MARQUIS, W.H. Grindley, Mark 59. Bread & Butter Plate, 6"d.

PLATE 185. MARTHA WASHINGTON, Royal Doulton, Mark 44. Plate, 10¼"d.

PLATE 186. MAZARA, William Adams & Co., Mark 7. Plate, 9"d.

PLATE 187. MEISSEN, Mark 137. Platter, 13½"l, 10"w.

PLATE 188. MELBOURNE, W.H. Grindley, Mark 60. Bowl, 9½"sq.

PLATE 189. MELROSE, Doulton, Mark 42. Plate, 8½"

PLATE 190. MERIAN, John Maddock, Marks 81 & 82. Soup Plate, 3"h, 11"d.

PLATE 191. "Messina," p. 118 (1st photograph), William Book I. Unmarked. Soup Bowl, 9"d.

PLATE 192. MILAN, Ford & Sons, Mark 51. Gravy Boat, 6½"l, Underplate, 8½"l.

PLATE 193. MONARCH, New Wharf Pottery Mark 98. Plate, 9"d.

PLATE 194. MONGOLIA, Johnson Bros., Mark 73. Platter, 11″l, 8″w.

PLATE 195. MONGOLIA, Johnson Bros., Mark 73. Covered Vegetable, 8″h, 11½″d. Pattern on inside of bowl also.

PLATE 196. "Muriel," p. 155, Williams' Book I. Unmarked. Bowl, 10″d.

PLATE 197. NAPIER, Keeling & Co., Mark 78. Wash Set: Toothbrush, 5¼″h; Chamber Pot, 6″h, 9″d; Covered Soap Dish, 4″h, 6″d, Polychromed.

PLATE 198. NAPIER, Keeling & Co., Mark 78. Wash Set: Bowl, 17″d; Pitcher, 9½″h, Polychromed.

PLATE 199. NATAL, Hollinshead & Kirkham, Mark 67. Plate, 10"d.

PLATE 200. NELSON, Grimwades, Mark 58. Soup Plate, 9"d.

PLATE 201. NON PAREIL, Burgess & Leigh, Mark 25. Plate, 8"d.

PLATE 202. NON PAREIL, Burgess & Leigh, Mark 25. Cup, 2¼"h; Saucer 5½"d. Note that borders are the same but scenes are different in the four examples shown of this pattern.

PLATE 203. NON PAREIL, Burgess & Leigh, Mark 25. Platter, 11¼″l.

PLATE 204. NON PAREIL, Burgess & Leigh, Mark 25. Cake Plate, 11″d.

PLATE 205. NORBURY, Royal Doulton, Mark 44. Spoonholder, 6″h.

PLATE 206. NORMANDY, Johnson Bros., Mark 71. Cup, 2½″h, Saucer, 4″d.

PLATE 208. OPHIR, Bourne & Leigh, Mark 21. Cup, 2¼″h, Saucer, 6″d.

PLATE 207. THE OLYMPIA, W.H. Grindley, Mark 61. Cup, 2¼″h, Saucer, 6″d.

PLATE 209. ORCHID, John Maddock and Sons, Mark 83. Pitcher, 7″h.

PLATE 210. OREGON, T.J. & J. Mayer, Mark 84. Plate, 8½"d.

PLATE 211. ORIENTAL, Ridgways, Mark 108. Platter, 19"l, 16"w.

PLATE 212. ORIENTAL, Ridgways, Mark 108. Creamer, 3½"h.

PLATE 213. ORIENTAL, L.A., Mark 79. Sauce Tureen, Polychromed on outer rim of lid.

PLATE 214. ORLEANS, Mark 138. Platter, 16"l, 14"w.

PLATE 215. "Ormonde," p. 209, Williams' Book I. J. & G. Meakin, Mark 90. Cup, 3"h; Saucer, 6"d.

PLATE 216. OSBORNE, W.H. Grindley, Mark 60. Oval Vegetable Bowl, 3½"h, 12½"l.

PLATE 217. OSBORNE, Ridgways, Mark 109. Soup Plate, 10"d.

PLATE 218. OSBORNE, Ridgways, Mark 109. Cup, 2½"h, Saucer, 6"d; Demi-tasse Cup, 2¼"h, Saucer, 4¼"d.

PLATE 219. OXFORD, Ford & Sons, Mark 51. Soup Plate, 10"d.

PLATE 220. OXFORD, Johnson Bros., Mark 70. Plate, 10"d.

PLATE 221. OXFORD, Johnson Bros., Mark 70. Berry Bowl, 5"d. Note no center pattern.

PLATE 222. PAGODA, J. & G. Meakin, Mark 90. Covered Vegetable, 10½"l.

PLATE 223. PAQUEMINOT, Ridgways, Mark 110. Plate, 10"d.

PLATE 224. PARIS, New Wharf Pottery, Mark 98. Plate, 9"d.

PLATE 225. PEACH, Johnson Bros., Mark 70. Berry Bowl, 5"d.

PLATE 226. "Pekin," p. 43, Williams' Book I. Marked "Albert E. Jones," circa 1905-1929. Plate, 9"d.

PLATE 227. PELEW, E. Challinor, Mark 30. Plate, 11"d.

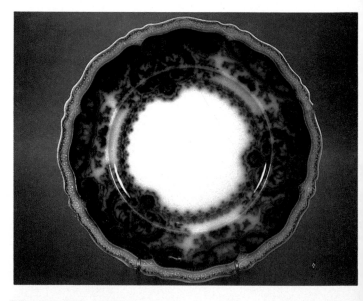

PLATE 228. PENANG, William Ridgway, Mark 107. Plate, 9¼"d.

PLATE 229. PERSIAN, Johnson Bros, Mark 70. Plate, 10"d.

PLATE 230. PERUVIAN, John Wedge Wood, Mark 130. 10½″d.

PLATE 231. PETUNIA, H. Bros., Mark 62. Hot Water jug with Liner, part of a wash set, 7¼″h.

PLATE 237. PROGRESS, W.H. Grindley, Mark 59. Berry Dish, 5″d.

PLATE 238. RALEIGH, Burgess & Leigh, Mark 27. Covered Vegetable Bowl, 11½″l.

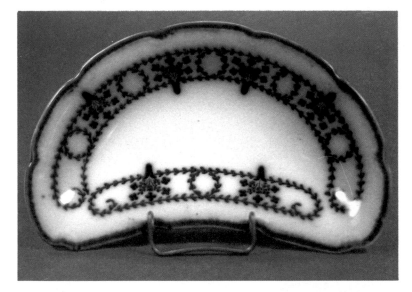

PLATE 239. THE REGAL, W.H. Grindley, Mark 61. Bone Dish, 6″d.

PLATE 240. REGINA, J. & G. Meakin, Mark 90. Soup Bowl, 9″d.

PLATE 241. RICHMOND, Johnson Bros., Mark 72. Berry Dish, 5½″d.

PLATE 242. ROSE, W.H. Grindley, Mark 60. Plate, 9″d

PLATE 243. ROSE, Myott, Son, & Co., Mark 96. Jardiniere, 7″h, 10″d.

PLATE 244. ROSE, Ridgways, Mark 110. Plate, 10″d.

PLATE 245. ROSEVILLE, John Maddock, Mark 83. Plate, 9″d.

PLATE 246. ROSEVILLE, John Maddock, Mark 83. Biscuit Jar, 8″h.

PLATE 247. ROXBURY, Ridgways, Mark 110. Creamer, 6″h.

PLATE 248. RUDYARD, F. Winkle & Co., Mark 128. Cover Sugar, 5½″h, Creamer, 6½″h.

PLATE 249. RUDYARD, F. Winkle & Co., Mark 128. Covered Butter, 5½″h, 7″d.

PLATE 250. RUSKIN, Ford & Sons, Mark 51. Plate 10″

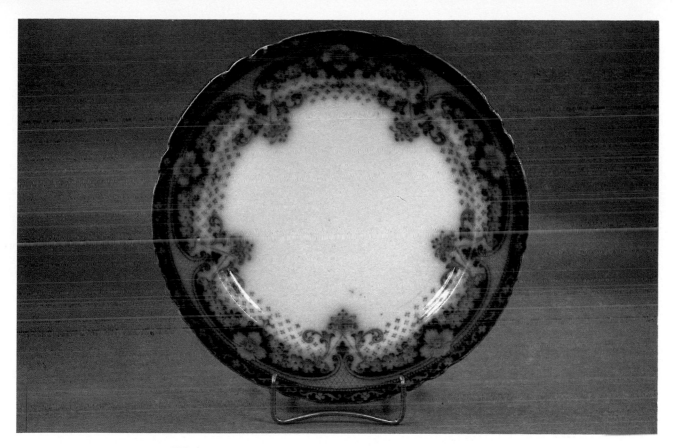

PLATE 251. SANDON, Ford & Sons, Mark 51. Plate, 10½″d.

PLATE 252. SASKIA, Ridgways, Mark 109. Mug, 3½″h; Pitcher, 8″h, Covered Soap Dish with Liner (not shown), 4″h, 5½″d.

PLATE 253. SAVOY, Johnson Bros., Mark 73. Sugar, cover missing, 5″h.

PLATE 254. SCINDE, John & George Alcock, Mark 13. Bread & Butter Plate, 7½″d.

PLATE 255. SEFTON, Ridgways, Mark 109. Berry Dish, 5½″d.

PLATE 256. SEVILLE, New Wharf Pottery, Mark 98. Cover Vegetable, 7″h, 12¼″l.

PLATE 257. SEVILLE, Wood & Son, Mark 131. Platter, 12½″l, 9″w.

PLATE 258. SEVILLE, Wood & Son, Mark 131. Covered Butter Dish, 5¼″h, 8″d.

PLATE 259. SHANGHAI, W.H. Grindley, Mark 60. Plate 10″d.

PLATE 260. SHANGHAI, W.H. Grindley, Mark 59. So▪ Plate, 9″d.

PLATE 262. "Shell," p. 199, Williams' Book I. Mark 1◄ Plate 8½″d.

PLATE 261. SHAPOO, Thomas Hughes, Mark 69. Cup 2¼″h; Saucer, 4½″d.

PLATE 263. "Simla," p. 50, Williams' Book I. Unmarked, Cup, 3″h.

PLATE 264. SIMLAY, Mark 140. Plate, 10½″d, Polychromed.

PLATE 265. SOBRAON, Mark 139. Plate, 10½″d.

PLATE 266. SOL, J. & G. Meakin, Mark 91. Covered Vegetable Bowl, 7½″h, 10½″l.

PLATE 267. SOMERSET, W.H. Grindley, Mark 61. Platter, 16½″l, 12½″w.

PLATE 268. STERLING, New Wharf Pottery, Mark 98. Vegetable Bowl, 3″h, 9″d.

PLATE 269. STERLING, Johnson Bros., Mark 73. Plate, 10″d.

PLATE 270. ST. LOUIS, Johnson Bros., Mark 70. Plate, ″d.

PLATE 271. SYDNEY, Wood & Son, Mark 132. Cup, 2¼″h.

PLATE 272. SYRIAN, W.H. Grindley, Mark 60. Wash Set: Bowl, 18″d; Pitcher, 11½″h, Covered Soap Dish, 6″d; Toothbrush, 5¼″h.

PLATE 273. SYRIAN, W.H. Grindley, Mark 60. Covered Waste Jar, 16″h overall.

PLATE 274. THE TEMPLE, Podmore, Walker, & Co., Mark 103. Plate, 10"d.

PLATE 275. THEODORE ROOSEVELT, Mark 111. Plate, 10"d.

PLATE 276. TOGO, F. Winkle & Co., Mark 129. Plate, 9"d.

PLATE 277. TONQUIN, Clementson & Young, Mark 32. Platter, 18"l, 14"w.

PLATE 278. TONQUIN, J. Heath, Mark 66. Plate, 9¼″d.

PLATE 279. TOURAINE, Stanley Pottery Co., Mark 113. Plate, 8″d.

PLATE 280. TOURAINE, Henry Alcock & Co., Mark 11. Vegetable Bowl, 3″h, 10½″d.

PLATE 281. TOURAINE, Henry Alcock & Co., Mark 11. Individual Fish or Bacon Platter, 6″l.

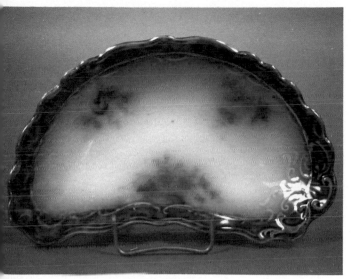

PLATE 282. TOURAINE, Henry Alcock & Co., Mark 11. Bone Dish, 6"l.

PLATE 283. TOURAINE, Henry Alcock & Co., Mark 11. Soup Plate, 9"d.

PLATE 284. TOURAINE, Henry Alcock & Co., Mark 11. Covered Sugar, 7½"h, Creamer, 5"h.

PLATE 285. TOURAINE, Henry Alcock & Co., Mark 11. Creamer, 4½"h.

PLATE 286. TOURAINE, Unmarked. Butter Pat, 3"d.

PLATE 287. TRENT, New Wharf Pottery, Mark 100. Plate, 10"d.

PLATE 289. TRILBY, Wood & Son, Mark 131. Vegetabl
Bowl, 9½″d.

PLATE 288. TRENTHAM, T. Rathbone &
Co., Mark 105. Pitcher, 9″h.

PLATE 290. TULIP, Johnson Bros., Mark 70. Covered
Vegetable Bowl, 6″h, 10″l.

PLATE 291. TURIN, Johnson Bros., Mark 73. Platte
12½″l, 9½″w.

PLATE 292. TURKEY, Ridgways, Mark 108. Plate, 10¼"d.

PLATE 293. VENICE, Grimwade Bros., Mark 56. Chamber Pot, 5½"h, 9½"w.

PLATE 294. VENICE, Upper Hanley Pottery, Mark 115. Plate, 10"d.

PLATE 295. VERMONT, Burgess & Leigh, Mark 26. Soup Plate, 9"d.

PLATE 296. VERNON, Doulton, Mark 43. Punch Bowl, 9″h, 14½″d.

PLATE 297. VERONA, Ridgways, Mark 110. Platter, 12½″l, 9½″w.

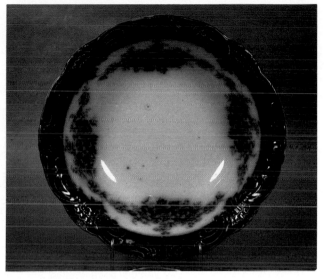

PLATE 298. VERSAILLES, T. Furnival & Sons, impressed an-chor and sword mark, circa 1878-1890. Covered Vegetable Bowl.

PLATE 299. VICTORIA, Wood & Son, Mark 131. Vegetable Bowl, 2½"h, 10"d.

PLATE 300. VIRGINIA, Doulton, Mark 42. Plate, 8"d.

PLATE 301. VISTA, G.L. Ashworth & Bros., Mark 19. Plate, 10¼"d.

PLATE 302. WALDORF, New Wharf Pottery, Mark 98. Plate, 10"d.

PLATE 303. WALDORF, New Wharf Pottery, Mark 98. Platter, 11"l, 9"w.

PLATE 304. WATTEAU, example is unmarked, but pattern is the same as border in Plate 305. Egg Holder, 6"h, 4½"sq.

PLATE 305. WATTEAU, Mark 141. Plate, 10"d.

PLATE 306. WATTEAU, Doulton, Mark 46. Rectangular Vegetable Bowl, 12"l.

PLATE 307. WATTEAU. Top to Vegetable Bowl in Pla[te] 306.

PLATE 308. WATTEAU, Doulton, Mark 47. Berry Dish, 5½"d. Note Doulton "Watteau" scenes are different in the four examples shown.

PLATE 309. WATTEAU. Doulton, Mark 46. Chocolate Pot, 8"h.

124

PLATE 310. WAVERLY, W.H. Grindley, Mark 60. Gravy Boat, 7"l.

PLATE 311. WEIR, Ford & Sons, Mark 52 with "England." Gravy Boat, 8"l.

PLATE 312. WELBECK, Sampson Hancock & Sons, Mark 64. Covered Vegetable Bowl, 10"l.

PLATE 313. WILD ROSE, George Jones & Sons, Mark 76. Creamer, 4"h.

PLATE 314. WILLOW, Doulton, Mark 40. Plate, 9½"d.

PLATE 315. WILLOW, Doulton, Mark 41. Cake Stand, 3¼"h, 9"d.

PLATE 316. WILLOW, Doulton, Mark 42. Creamers, 4¼"h & 4½"h.

PLATE 317. WILLOW, Doulton, Mark 4. Waste Bowl, 3¼"h, 6½"d.

PLATE 318. WILLOW, Doulton, Mark 42. Chamber Pot, 5½"h, 9¼"d.

PLATE 319. WILLOW, Doulton, Mark 42. Bowl and Pitcher Set.

PLATE 320. WINDFLOWER, Burgess
& Leigh, Mark 26. Plate, 10″d.

PLATE 321. YEDDO, Arthur J. Wilkinson, Mark 125. Soup Bowl, 7½″d.

PLATE 322. YEDO, G.L. Ashworth,
Mark 17. Footed Platter, 13″l, 9″w.

Unidentified Patterns

PLATE 324. Biscuit Jar, unmarked.

PLATE 323. Biscuit Jar, "Made in England," impressed mark.

PLATE 325. Bone Dish, 6"l, marked "England."

PLATE 326. Butter Dish, J. & G. Meakin, Mark 88. See Plates 334 and 350 for same pattern.

PLATE 327. Butter Pat, 3½"d, unmarked.

PLATE 328. Butter Pat, 3"d, marked with initials "F.B."

PLATE 329. Cake Plate, 8½"d, marked with impressed initials "G.G."

PLATE 330. Cake Plate, 10"sq, marked "Balmoral China" over figure of a lion, company unidentified.

PLATE 331. Cheese Dish, Wiltshaw & Robinson, Mark 127.

PLATE 332. Cheese Dish, 9½"h, 9"d, Doulton, Mark 43.

PLATE 333. Chocolate Pot, 6"h, unmarked.

PLATE 334. Coffee Pot, J. & G. Meakin, Mark 88. See Plates 326 and 350 for same pattern.

PLATE 335. Handleless Cup, 3″h, Josiah Wedgwood, Mark 124.

PLATE 336. Cup, 3¼″h, unmarked.

PLATE 337. Cup, 3½″h, unmarked.

PLATE 338. Cup, 3″h, unmarked.

PLATE 339. Cup, 3″h, unmarked.

PLATE 340. Cup, 2½″h, unmarked.

PLATE 341. Cup, 2″h; Saucer, 6″d, unmarked.

PLATE 342. Cup, 3″h; Saucer, 6″d, unmarked.

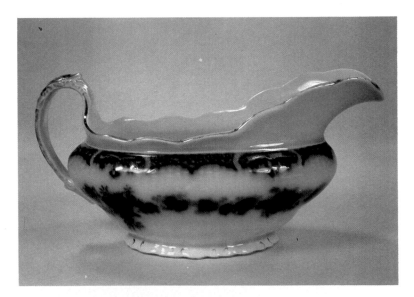

PLATE 343. Gravy Boat, 3″h, 8″l, mark illegible.

PLATE 344. Pitcher, 12″h, unmarked Polychromed.

PLATE 345. Pitcher, 8″h, Doulton, Mark 44.   PLATE 346. Pitcher, 8½″h, unmarked.

PLATE 347. Pitcher, 7″h, Samuel Johnson,   PLATE 348. Pitcher, 12″h, Doulton, Mark 42.
Mark 74, Polychromed, pewter lid.

133

PLATE 349. Pitcher, 6″h. "ENGLAND" incised mark, printed mark unclear.

PLATE 350. Pitcher, 7¼"h, J. & G. Meakin, Mark 88, see Plates 326 and 334 for same pattern.

PLATE 351. Pitcher, 13"h, Minton, "B.B." impressed, see Mark 94.

PLATE 352. Pitcher and Trivet, Wiltshaw & Robinson, Mark 127. See Plate 366 for same pattern.

PLATE 353. Pitcher, 11"h, unmarked.

PLATE 354. Plate, 9¼″d, unmarked, Antelope.

PLATE 355. Plates, 9½″d, Doulton, Mark 44. Game Birds, pair from set of six, each with different game birds.

PLATE 356. Plates, 9½″d, unmarked, Turkeys.

PLATE 357. Plate, 10″d, unmarked.

PLATE 358. Plate, 9″d, Keeling & Co., Mark 77.

PLATE 359. Plate, 10½″d, Doulton, Mark 42.

PLATE 360. Plate, 10″d, Josiah Wedgwood, Mark 124.

PLATE 361. Plate, 10″d, Mark 142.

PLATE 362. Relish, 6½″l, W. Adams & Co., Mark 3.

PLATE 363. Relish, 11½″d, Doulton, Mark 42.

PLATE 364. Covered Sugar, 8½″h, unmarked. See Plate 365 for same pattern.

PLATE 365. Teapot, 9½″h, unmarked. See Plate 364 for same pattern.

PLATE 366. Teapot, 7″h, and Trivet, 5″d, Wiltshaw & Robinson, Mark 127. See Plate 352 for this same pattern.

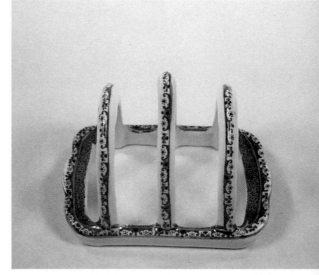

PLATE 367. Toast Rack, 4″h, unmarked.

LATE 368. Tureen, Marked "CAULDON, ENGLAND," olychromned.

PLATE 369. Tureen, 12″h, 16″w, unmarked.

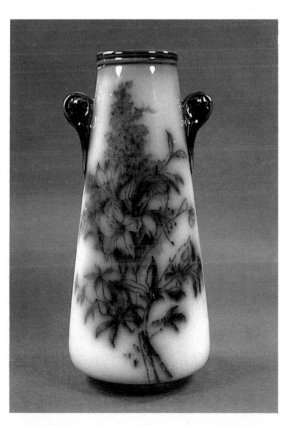

PLATE 370. Vase, 13″h, unmarked. See Plate 434 for a new mold copy of this piece.

PLATE 371. Vase, 11″h, mark illegible.

PLATE 372. Vegetable Bowl, 10″d, unmarked.

PLATE 373. Vegetable Bowl, 10″d, unmarked.

PLATE 374. Wash Set: Bowl, 16″d; Pitcher, 13″h, Wiltshaw & Robinson, Mark 127. Border is like that of PETUNIA, see Plate 232.

PLATE 375. Wash Set: Bowl, 15″d; Pitcher, 13″h; Covered Soap Dish with Liner, 6½″l; Flat Toothbrush Holder, 9″l, 4½″w, unmarked.

PLATE 376. Wash Set: Bowl, 16″d; Pitcher, 11½″h, unmarked.

PLATE 377. Wash Set: Chamber Pot, Doulton, Mark 42.

PLATE 378. Wash Set: Chamber Pot with Lid, W.H. Grindley, Mark 60.

PLATE 380. Wash Set: Toothbrush Holder, 5½"h, unmarked. Matches set in Plate 376.

PLATE 379. Wash Set: Toothbrush Holder, 5"h, Burgess & Leigh, Mark 26.

PLATE 381. Wash Set: Flat Tooth Brush Holder, 9"l, 4"w; Covered Soap Dish with Drainer, 6"l, 5"w, unmarked.

PLATE 382. Wash Set: Toothbrush Holder, 5½"h, unmarked.

Handpainted Flow Blue

PLATE 383. Waste Bowl, 3½″h, 5½″w, unmarked, copper lustre.

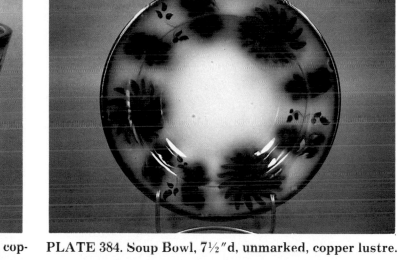

PLATE 384. Soup Bowl, 7½″d, unmarked, copper lustre.

PLATE 385. Waste Bowl to Child's Set, 2½″h, 4½″d, unmarked, copper lustre.

PLATE 386. Shaving Mug, 3¼″h, unmarked, copper lustre.

PLATE 387. Child's Set: Cup, 2½″h; Saucer, 4½″d, unmarked, copper lustre.

PLATE 388. Shaving Mug, 3″h, unmarked, copper lustre.

PLATE 389. Pitcher, 6½″h, Charles Allerton & Sons, Mark 15, copper lustre.

PLATE 390. Pitcher, 8½"h, unmarked, copper lustre.

PLATE 391. Cake Plate, 9¼″sq, unmarked, copper lustre.

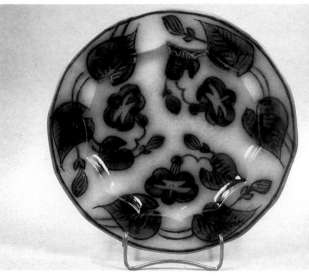

PLATE 392. Plate, 9¼″d, unmarked, copper lustre.

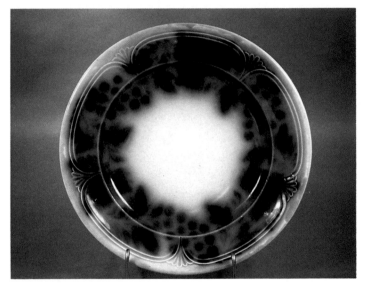

PLATE 393. Plate, 8½″d, Edward Walley, Mark 119.

PLATE 394. Handleless cup, 3″h; Saucer, 6″d, unmarked, polychromed.

PLATE 395. Cup, 2¼″h; Saucer, 6″d, unmarked, polychromed.

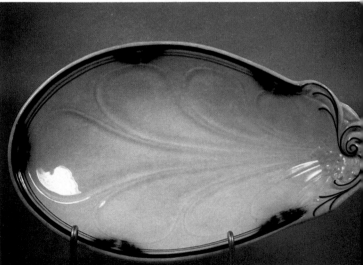

PLATE 396. Relish, 8½″l, unmarked, polychromed.

Non-English Flow Blue

PLATE 397. Bowl, 3½"h, 9"d, marked "Victoria, Austria" with an embossed crown shape. Mark of Schmidt & Co., after 1883.

PLATE 398. Bread & Butter Plate, 7½"d, Jean Pouyat, Limoges, France, Mark 144.

PLATE 399. Fruit Bowl, 4½"d, handpainted, Utzchneider & Co., France, Mark 146.

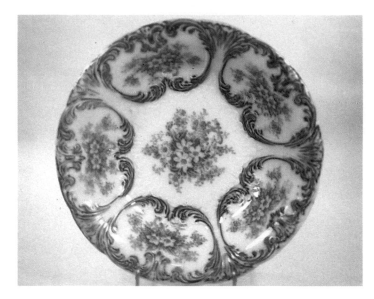

PLATE 400. Bowl, 10″d, MEISSEN pattern, F.A. Mehlem, Germany, Mark 149.

PLATE 401. Cup, 2½″h; Saucer, 6½″d, JARDINIERE pattern, Villeroy & Boch, Germany, Mark 151.

PLATE 402. Plate, 8¼″d, pattern QUEBEC, Germany, Mark 147.

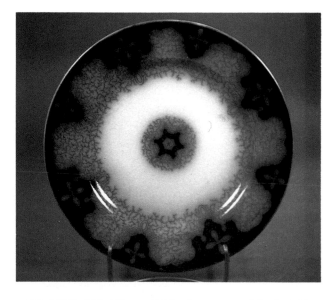

PLATE 403. Plate, 8″d, Germany, Mark 148.

PLATE 404. Plate, 9½″d, FASAN pattern, Villeroy & Boch, Germany, Mark 152.

PLATE 405. Plate, 9″d, HONC pattern, Petrus Regout, Holland, Mark 153.

PLATE 406. Plate, 9″d, Petrus Regout, Holland, Mark 153, SUPERIOR pattern.

PLATE 407. Bowl, 9¼″d, handpainted, Societe Ceramique, Holland, mark 154.

PLATE 408. Plate, 9″d, "T.A." in floral shape, Japan, Mark 155.

150

PLATE 409. Cup, 2"h; Saucer, 5½"d, Gilman & Co., Portugal, Mark 156.

PLATE 410. Plate, 7¼"d, handpainted, Prussia, Mark 157.

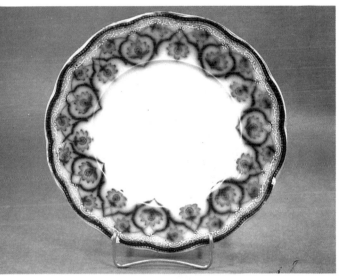

PLATE 411. Plate, 9"d, Prussia, Mark 157.

PLATE 412. Trinket Box, 4"l, Reinhold Schlegelmilch, Tillowitz, Prussia, steeple mark, circa mid 1870's-1880.

PLATE 413. Soup Bowl, 9"d, ROYAL BLUE pattern, Burgess & Campbell, U.S., Mark 158. The same pattern on a 10" plate has BALMORAL as pattern name, see Marks 159 and 160.

PLATE 414. Covered Bowl, 7½"h, 12½"l, The Colonial Company, Mark 161.

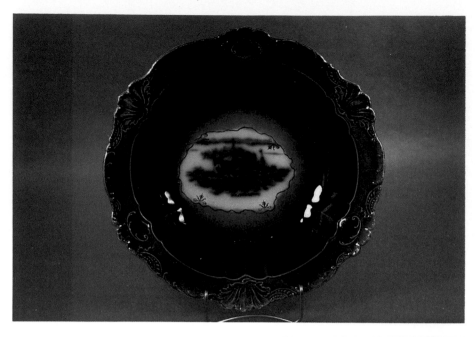

PLATE 415. Bowl, 11″d, U.S.S. Brooklyn, The French China Co., U.S., Mark 163.

PLATE 416. Oval Bowl, 13″l, 9½″w, U.S.S. MAINE, The French China Co., U.S., Mark 163.

PLATE 417. Pitcher, 5″h, The French China Co., U.S. Mark 162.

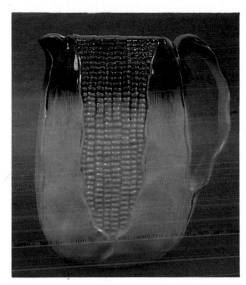

PLATE 418. Pitcher, 8″h, The French China Co., U.S., Mark 163.

PLATE 419. Fruit Bowl, 5¼″d, The French China Co., U.S. Mark 162.

PLATE 420. Pitcher, 7″h, ARGYLE pattern, J. & E. Mayer, U.S. Mark 164.

PLATE 421. Oval Bowl, 9½″l, VERNON pattern, Mellor & Co., U.S. Mark 165.

PLATE 422. Butter Pat, 3″d, Mercer Pottery Co., U.S., Mark 166.

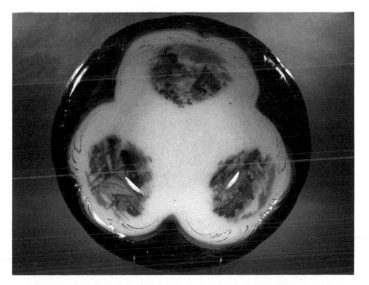

PLATE 423. Bowl to Wash Set 17″d, DELPH pattern, marked "The Sebring." Sebring Pottery Co., Sebring, Ohio, U.S., circa 1887-mid 1930's.

153

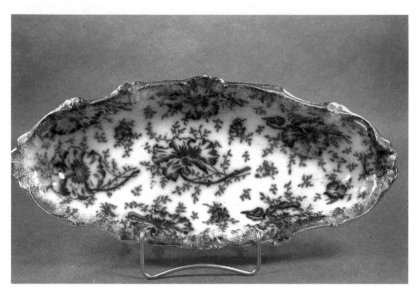

PLATE 424. Relish, 12¼″l, 5½″w, marked "Warwick China."

PLATE 425. Molasses Pitcher, 4″h, pewter top, marked "Warwick China." The Warwich China Co., Wheeling, West Virginia, U.S., after 1898.

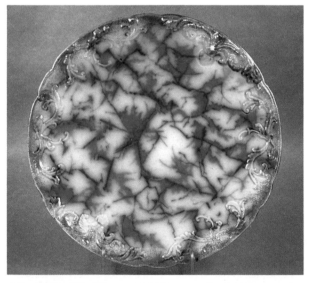

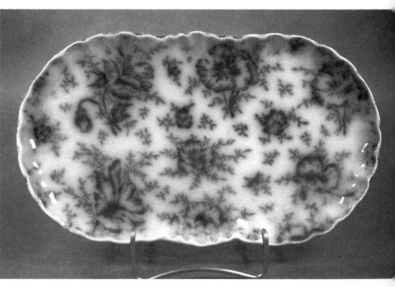

PLATE 426. Plate, 10½″d, marked "Warwick China."

PLATE 427. Tray, 10½″l, 6″w, marked "Warwick China."

PLATE 428. Plate with place for cup, 8¼"d, LA BELLE, Mark 167.

PLATE 429. Bread & Butter Plate, 7½"d, Wheeling Pottery Co., U.S. Mark 167. This pattern is popularly called "LA BELLE" because of the company mark although other patterns also have the same mark.

PLATE 430. Footed Bowl, 6"h, 13"l, 11"w, LA BELLE, Mark 168.

PLATE 431. Pitcher, 7"h, LA BELLE, Mark 167.

PLATE 432. Oblong Bowl, 11¼"l, 9"w, LA BELLE, Mark 168.

PLATE 433. Bowl, 3"h, 11"d, LA BELLE, Mark 168.

155

New Flow Blue

PLATE 434. New Flow Blue Vase. See Plate 370 to see that the new piece differs in body mold only in the fancy handles. New piece is unmarked.

PLATE 435. New Mark found on many new Flow Blue items decorated as the example in next plate (436). It is one mark used by the Blakeney Pottery Company, Stoke-on-Trent, England on their "Flow Blue" wares.

PLATE 436. New Flow Blue Covered Dish, Blakeney Pottery, marked with mark shown in Plate 435.

Value Guide

Prices for Flow Blue patterns and objects featured in this book show a range of prices for each item. Prices quoted are for pieces in mint condition. Many factors determine the ultimate price of an item, including condition, scarcity, and the individual buyer's desire for a particular pattern or piece of Flow Blue. Prices listed for Flow Blue in this book were based on current prices asked or received by dealers and collectors in this field. Every effort has been made to present as accurate an indication of value as possible. Please remember, however, THAT THE PRICES ARE INTENDED TO BE USED ONLY AS A GUIDE. Prices for patterns and objects may be found well above and below the range quoted here.

In order to find a price range for various objects and patterns which are not found in this book, please consult the Object Index. One can compare prices for specific objects and patterns. It is not possible, of course, to list a price for all of the different pieces made in all of the patterns presented in this book or to show all of the specific Flow Blue patterns that have ever been made. If you have a covered vegetable bowl, for example, but one is not shown in your pattern, you may be able to get a good estimate of the price range by comparing prices for covered vegetable bowls in other patterns. Look for similar patterns and manufacturers and compare the price relationships between types of objects. Although this is by no means a precise way to estimate prices, it does provide some guidance.

Plate 1 . . . .$70.00-$80.00	Plate 30 . . . . . .$50.00-$60.00	Plate 58 . . . .$120.00-$140.00	Plate 87 . . . . .$50.00-$60.00
Plate 2 . . . . . .$75.00-$85.00	Plate 31 . . . . . .$45.00-$55.00	Plate 59 . . . . .$80.00-$100.00	Plate 88 . . . . .$60.00-$70.00
Plate 3 Set $650.00-750.00	Plate 32 . . . .$100.00-$120.00	Plate 60 . . . . .$80.00-$100.00	Plate 89 . . . . .$50.00-$60.00
Plate 4 . . . . . .$80.00-$100.00	Plate 33 . . . . . .$55.00-$65.00	Plate 61 . . . .$350.00-$450.00	Plate 90 . . . . $50.00-$60.00
Plate 5 . . . . . .$20.00-$25.00	Plate 34 . . . . .$80.00-$100.00	Plate 62 . . . .$250.00-$300.00	Plate 91 . . . .$300.00-$400.00
Plate 6 . . . . .$175.00-$200.00	Plate 35 . . . .$250.00-$300.00	Plate 63 Each . . . . . .$100.00-$120.00	Plate 92 . . . . .$35.00-$45.00
Plate 7 . . . . . .$80.00-$100.00	Plate 36 . . . .$130.00-$140.00	Plate 64 . . . .$500.00-$600.00	Plate 93 . . . .$130.00-$150.00
Plate 8 . . . . . .$40.00-$50.00	Plate 37 . . . . .$80.00-$100.00	Plate 65 . . . .$350.00-$450.00	Plate 94 . . . .$140.00-$160.00
Plate 9 . . . .$200.00-$250.00	Plate 38 . . . . . .$50.00-$60.00	Plate 66 . . . . . .$70.00-$80.00	Plate 95 . . . . .$20.00-$25.00
Plate 10 . . . . .$90.00-$100.00	Plate 39 . . . . . .$60.00-$70.00	Plate 67 . . . .$550.00-$650.00	Plate 96 . . . . .$80.00-$100.00
Plate 11 . . . . . .$60.00-$70.00	Plate 40 . . . .$140.00-$150.00	Plate 68 . . . .$225.00-$275.00	Plate 97 . . . . .$70.00-$90.00
Plate 12 . . . .$110.00-$130.00	Plate 41 . . . . . .$35.00-$40.00	Plate 69 . . . . .$70.00-$80.00	Plate 98 . . . . .$80.00-$100.00
Plate 13 . . . .$100.00-$120.00	Plate 42 . . . .$200.00-$250.00	Plate 70 . . . . .$40.00-$50.00	Plate 99 . . . . .$35.00-$45.00
Plate 14 . . . . . .$50.00-$60.00	Plate 43 . . . .$150.00-$175.00	Plate 71 . . . .$250.00-$300.00	Plate 100 . . . . .$40.00-$50.00
Plate 15 . . . .$110.00-$130.00	Plate 44 . . . .$150.00-$175.00	Plate 72 . . . .$140.00-$160.00	Plate 101 . . .$150.00-$170.00
Plate 16 . . . .$110.00-$130.00	Plate 45 . . . . . .$75.00-$85.00	Plate 73 . . . . . .$50.00-$60.00	Plate 102 . . .$130.00-$150.00
Plate 17 . . . .$100.00-$120.00	Plate 46 . . . . . .$40.00-$50.00	Plate 74 . . . . . .$40.00-$50.00	Plate 103 . . .$150.00-$175.00
Plate 18 . . . .$200.00-$225.00	Plate 47 . . . . . .$60.00-$70.00	Plate 75 . . . .$100.00-$125.00	Plate 104 . . .$100.00-$125.00
Plate 19 . . . . .$55.00-$65.00	Plate 48 . . . .$100.00-$125.00	Plate 76 . . . . . .$70.00-$80.00	Plate 105 . . .$175.00-$200.00
Plate 20 . . . .$100.00-$125.00	Plate 49 . . . . . .$45.00-$55.00	Plate 77 . . . .$150.00-$175.00	Plate 106 . . . . .$25.00-$30.00
Plate 21 . . . . .$55.00-$65.00	Plate 50 . . . . .$80.00-$100.00	Plate 78 . . . .$250.00-$300.00	Plate 107 . . .$100.00-$120.00
Plate 22 . . . . .$50.00-$60.00	Plate 51 . . . .$250.00-$300.00	Plate 79 . . . .$250.00-$300.00	Plate 108 . . . . .$75.00-$85.00
Plate 23 . . . .$100.00-$120.00	Plate 52 . . . . . .$55.00-$65.00	Plate 80 . . . . . .$50.00-$60.00	Plate 109 . . . . .$50.00-$60.00
Plate 24 . . . . . .$55.00-$65.00	Plate 53 . . . . . .$65.00-$75.00	Plate 81 . . . .$100.00-$120.00	Plate 110 . . .$150.00-$175.00
Plate 25 . . . . .$55.00-$65.00	Plate 54 . . . . . .$45.00-$55.00	Plate 82 . . . . .$80.00-$100.00	Plate 111 . . . . .$65.00-$75.00
Plate 26 . . . . .$35.00-$45.00	Plate 55 Set . . . .$500.00-$600.00	Plate 83 . . . . .$30.00-$35.00	Plate 112 . . .$100.00-$120.00
Plate 27 . . . . .$40.00-$50.00	Plate 56 . . . . . . .see Plate 55	Plate 84 . . . .$80.00-$100.00	Plate 113 . . . . .$65.00-$75.00
Plate 28 . . . . .$55.00-$65.00	Plate 57 Plate . . . .$50.00-$60.00 Cup/Saucer . . .$55.00-$65.00	Plate 85 . . . . . .$35.00-$45.00	Plate 114 . . .$175.00-$200.00
Plate 29 Set . . . .$750.00-$850.00		Plate 86 . . . .$100.00-$120.00	Plate 115 . . . . .$45.00-$55.00

157

Plate 116 . . . . . $45.00-$55.00	Plate 156 . . . $100.00-$120.00	Plate 195 . . . $200.00-$250.00	Plate 234 . . . . $80.00-$100.00
Plate 117 . . . . . $45.00-$55.00	Plate 157 . . . $175.00-$200.00	Plate 196 . . . . $55.00-$65.00	Plate 235 . . . $80.00-$100.00
Plate 118 . . $800.00-$1,000.00	Plate 158 . . . . $55.00-$65.00	**Plate 197**	Plate 236 . . . $150.00-$175.00
Plate 119 . . . . . $45.00-$55.00	Plate 159 . . . . $45.00-$55.00	Set . . . . $800.00-$1,000.00	Plate 237 . . . . $15.00-$20.00
Plate 120 . . . . . $45.00-$55.00	Plate 160 . . . $150.00-$170.00	Plate 198 . . . . . see Plate 197	Plate 238 . . $225.00-$250.00
Plate 121 . . . $250.00-$300.00	Plate 161 . . . . $45.00-$55.00	Plate 199 . . . . $45.00-$55.00	Plate 239 . . . . $30.00-$35.00
Plate 122 . . . . . $55.00-$65.00	Plate 162 . . . . $15.00-$20.00	Plate 200 . . . . $40.00-$50.00	Plate 240 . . . . $50.00-$60.00
Plate 123 . . $100.00-$125.00	Plate 163 . . . $100.00-$120.00	Plate 201 . . . . $60.00-$80.00	Plate 241 . . . . $20.00-$25.00
Plate 124 . . . $150.00-$175.00	Plate 164 . . . $150.00-$175.00	Plate 202 . . . . $65.00-$85.00	Plate 242 . . . . $40.00-$50.00
Plate 125 . . . . . $50.00-$60.00	Plate 165 . . . . $70.00-$90.00	Plate 203 . . $200.00-$250.00	Plate 243 . . $225.00-$275.00
Plate 126 . . $100.00-$120.00	Plate 166 . . . . $60.00-$70.00	Plate 204 . . . $150.00-$175.00	Plate 244 . . . . $50.00-$60.00
Plate 127 . . $100.00-$125.00	Plate 167 . . . . $70.00-$90.00	Plate 205 . . . $150.00-$175.00	Plate 245 . . . . $45.00-$55.00
Plate 128 . . $125.00-$150.00	Plate 168 . . . . $40.00-$50.00	Plate 206 . . . . $60.00-$70.00	Plate 246 . . $150.00-$175.00
Plate 129 . . . . $40.00-$50.00	Plate 169 . . . . $20.00-$25.00	Plate 207 . . . . $50.00-$60.00	Plate 247 . . $130.00-$150.00
Plate 130 . . $110.00-$130.00	Plate 170 . . . . $55.00-$65.00	Plate 208 . . . . $65.00-$75.00	**Plate 248**
Plate 131 . . $100.00-$125.00	Plate 171 . . . . $55.00-$65.00	Plate 209 . . $200.00-$225.00	Set $150.00-175.00
Plate 132 . . . . $80.00-$100.00	Plate 172 . . . . $80.00-$100.00	Plate 210 . . . . $80.00-$100.00	Plate 249 . . $150.00-$175.00
Plate 133 . . . $250.00-$275.00	Plate 173 . . $225.00-$275.00	Plate 211 . . $250.00-$300.00	Plate 250 . . . . $80.00-$100.00
Plate 134 . . . . . $55.00-$65.00	Plate 174 . . $250.00-$300.00	Plate 212 . . . . $75.00-$100.00	Plate 251 . . . . . $50.00-$60.00
Plate 135 . . . $150.00-$175.00	**Plate 175**	Plate 213 . . $150.00-$175.00	**Plate 252**
Plate 136 . . . . $80.00-$90.00	8½" h . . . . . $225.00-$275.00	Plate 214 . . $125.00-$150.00	Cup . . . . $50.00-$60.00
Plate 137 . . . . . $30.00-$35.00	7" h . . . . . . $200.00-$250.00	Plate 215 . . . . $60.00-$70.00	Pitcher . . . . $200.00-$225.00
Plate 138 . . . $80.00-$100.00	Plate 176 . . . . $45.00-$55.00	Plate 216 . . . $80.00-$100.00	Soap Dish . . $150.00-$175.00
Plate 139 . . . $65.00-$75.00	Plate 177 . . . . $60.00-$80.00	Plate 217 . . . . . $45.00-$55.00	Plate 253 . . . . $60.00-$70.00
Plate 140 . . $100.00-$125.00	Plate 178 . . . . $45.00-$55.00	**Plate 218**	Plate 254 . . . . $60.00-$70.00
Plate 141 . . $150.00-$175.00	Plate 179 . . $120.00-$140.00	Cup/saucer . . . $60.00-$70.00	Plate 255 . . . . $20.00-$25.00
Plate 142 . . . . . $12.00-$15.00	Plate 180 . . $100.00-$125.00	Demi-tasse . . . $65.00-$75.00	Plate 256 . . $250.00-$275.00
Plate 143 . . . . . $45.00-$55.00	Plate 181 . . . . $45.00-$55.00	Plate 219 . . . . $55.00-$65.00	Plate 257 . . . $175.00-$200.00
Plate 144 . . . . . $50.00-$60.00	Plate 182 . . . . $30.00-$40.00	Plate 220 . . . . $50.00-$60.00	Plate 258 . . $200.00-$250.00
Plate 145 . . . . . $60.00-$70.00	Plate 183 . . . . $30.00-$40.00	Plate 221 . . . . . $25.00-$30.00	Plate 259 . . . $80.00-$100.00
Plate 146 . . . . . $45.00-$55.00	Plate 184 . . . . $30.00-$35.00	Plate 222 . . $200.00-$225.00	Plate 260 . . . $80.00-$100.00
Plate 147 . . . . . $70.00-$80.00	Plate 185 . . . . $65.00-$75.00	Plate 223 . . . . $45.00-$55.00	Plate 261 . . . . . $55.00-$65.00
Plate 148 . . . . . $25.00-$30.00	Plate 186 . . . . $60.00-$80.00	Plate 224 . . . . $55.00-$65.00	Plate 262 . . . . $60.00-$70.00
Plate 149 . . $125.00-$150.00	Plate 187 . . $150.00-$200.00	Plate 225 . . . . $20.00-$25.00	Plate 263 . . . $80.00-$100.00
Plate 150 . . . . $80.00-$100.00	Plate 188 . . . . $60.00-$80.00	Plate 226 . . . . $60.00-$70.00	Plate 264 . . . $80.00-$100.00
Plate 151 . . $100.00-$125.00	Plate 189 . . . . $45.00-$55.00	Plate 227 . . $110.00-$130.00	Plate 265 . . $100.00-$125.00
Plate 152 . . . $80.00-$100.00	Plate 190 . . $100.00-$120.00	Plate 228 . . $100.00-$125.00	Plate 266 . . $150.00-$175.00
Plate 153	Plate 191 . . . . $55.00-$65.00	Plate 229 . . . . $55.00-$65.00	Plate 267 . . $175.00-$200.00
Tureen . . . . . $225.00-$275.00	**Plate 192**	Plate 230 . . $100.00-$125.00	Plate 268 . . . . $65.00-$75.00
Ladle . . . . $80.00-$100.00	Set . . . . $125.00-$150.00	Plate 231 . . $225.00-$275.00	Plate 269 . . . . $50.00-$60.00
Plate 154 . . . . . $45.00-$55.00	Plate 193 . . . . $45.00-$55.00	Plate 232 . . $140.00-$160.00	Plate 270 . . . . . $50.00-$60.00
Plate 155 . . . . . $60.00-$70.00	Plate 194 . . $125.00-$150.00	Plate 233 . . . . $60.00-$80.00	Plate 271 . . . . . $45.00-$50.00
			Plate 272
			Set . . . . . $1,200.00-$1,500.00

Plate 273 . . . . . see Plate 272

Plate 274 . . . $100.00-$125.00

Plate 275 . . . . . $65.00-$75.00

Plate 276 . . . . . $60.00-$80.00

Plate 277 . . . $350.00-$400.00

Plate 278 . . . $100.00-$125.00

Plate 279 . . . . . $55.00-$65.00

Plate 280 . . . $120.00-$140.00

Plate 281 . . . . . $45.00-$55.00

Plate 282 . . . . . $45.00-$55.00

Plate 283 . . . . . $60.00-$70.00

Plate 284
Set . . . . $300.00-$325.00

Plate 285 . . . $140.00-$150.00

Plate 286 . . . . . $30.00-$35.00

Plate 287 . . . . . $50.00-$60.00

Plate 288 . . . $225.00-$275.00

Plate 289 . . . . . $60.00-$75.00

Plate 290 . . . $140.00-$160.00

Plate 291 . . . $100.00-$120.00

Plate 292 . . . . . $70.00-$80.00

Plate 293 . . . . $175.00-200.00

Plate 294 . . . . . $50.00-$60.00

Plate 295 . . . . . $45.00-$55.00

Plate 296 . . $800.00-$1,000.00

Plate 297 . . . $120.00-$140.00

Plate 298 . . . $150.00-$175.00

Plate 299 . . . . . $60.00-$70.00

Plate 300 . . . . . $40.00-$50.00

Plate 301 . . . $80.00-$100.00

Plate 302 . . . . . $60.00-$70.00

Plate 303 . . . $130.00-$150.00

Plate 304 . . . $150.00-$175.00

Plate 305 . . . . $80.00-$100.00

Plate 306 . . . $250.00-$275.00

Plate 307 . . . . . see Plate 306

Plate 308 . . . . . $35.00-$45.00

Plate 309 . . . $225.00-$275.00

Plate 310 . . . $80.00-$100.00

Plate 311 . . . . . $70.00-$90.00

Plate 312 . . . $125.00-$150.00

Plate 313 . . . $120.00-$140.00

Plate 314 . . . . . $60.00-$70.00

Plate 315 . . . $150.00-$175.00

Plate 316 . . . $100.00-$125.00

Plate 317 . . . . . $50.00-$60.00

Plate 318 . . . $200.00-$250.00

Plate 319
Set . . . . $600.00-$700.00

Plate 320 . . . . . $35.00-$45.00

Plate 321 . . . . . $55.00-$65.00

Plate 322 . . . $225.00-$250.00

Plate 323 . . . $150.00-$175.00

Plate 324 . . . $100.00-$125.00

Plate 325 . . . . . $50.00-$60.00

Plate 326 . . . $175.00-$200.00

Plate 327 . . . . . $20.00-$25.00

Plate 328 . . . . $20.00-$25.00

Plate 329 . . . . . $70.00-$80.00

Plate 330 . . . . . $70.00-$80.00

Plate 331 . . . $225.00-$250.00

Plate 332 . . . $200.00-$250.00

Plate 333 . . . $100.00-$125.00

Plate 334 . . . $175.00-$200.00

Plate 335 . . . . $90.00-$100.00

Plate 336 . . . . $80.00-$100.00

Plate 337 . . . . . $50.00-$60.00

Plate 338 . . . . . $60.00-$70.00

Plate 339 . . . . . $40.00-$50.00

Plate 340 . . . . . $45.00-$55.00

Plate 341 . . . . . $55.00-$65.00

Plate 342 . . . . . $60.00-$70.00

Plate 343 . . . . . $70.00-$90.00

Plate 344 . . . $150.00-$175.00

Plate 345 . . . $200.00-$225.00

Plate 346 . . . $150.00-$200.00

Plate 347 . . . $100.00-$125.00

Plate 348 . . . $225.00-$275.00

Plate 349 . . . $150.00-$175.00

Plate 350 . . . $160.00-$180.00

Plate 351 . . . $225.00-$250.00

Plate 352
Pitcher . . . . . $150.00-$175.00
Trivet . . . . $50.00-$60.00

Plate 353 . . . $175.00-$200.00

Plate 354 . . . . . $50.00-$60.00

Plate 355
Each . . . . $80.00-$100.00

Plate 356
Pair . . . . $130.00-$150.00

Plate 357 . . . . $80.00-$100.00

Plate 358 . . . . . $60.00-$70.00

Plate 359 . . . . $80.00-$100.00

Plate 360 . . . . . $70.00-$80.00

Plate 361 . . . . . $60.00-$70.00

Plate 362 . . . . . $45.00-$55.00

Plate 363 . . . . $80.00-$100.00

Plate 364 . . . $275.00-$300.00

Plate 365 . . . $300.00-$350.00

Plate 366
Teapot . . . . . $125.00-$150.00
Trivet . . . . $50.00-$60.00

Plate 367 . . . . $80.00-$100.00

Plate 368 . . . $400.00-$450.00

Plate 369
Set . . . . $500.00-$600.00

Plate 370 . . . $350.00-$400.00

Plate 371 . . . $300.00-$350.00

Plate 372 . . . . . $70.00-$80.00

Plate 373 . . . . $80.00-$100.00

Plate 374
Set . . . . $600.00-$700.00

Plate 375
Set . . . . $800.00-$900.00

Plate 376
Set . . . . $600.00-$700.00

Plate 377 . . . $175.00-$200.00

Plate 378 . . . $200.00-$250.00

Plate 379 . . . $150.00-$175.00

Plate 380 . . . $150.00-$175.00

Plate 381
Each item . . $200.00-$225.00

Plate 382 . . . . . $80.00-$90.00

Plate 383 . . . $125.00-$150.00

Plate 384 . . . . . $60.00-$70.00

Plate 385 . . . . . $70.00-$80.00

Plate 386 . . . $180.00-$200.00

Plate 387 . . . . $80.00-$100.00

Plate 388 . . . $180.00-$200.00

Plate 389 . . . $175.00-$200.00

Plate 390 . . . $200.00-$225.00

Plate 391 . . . $150.00-$160.00

Plate 392 . . . $125.00-$135.00

Plate 393 . . . . . $55.00-$65.00

Plate 394 . . . . $80.00-$100.00

Plate 395 . . . . . $70.00-$80.00

Plate 396 . . . . . $40.00-$50.00

Plate 397 . . . $125.00-$150.00

Plate 398 . . . . . $20.00-$30.00

Plate 399 . . . . . $25.00-$30.00

Plate 400 . . . . . $55.00-$65.00

Plate 401 . . . . . $65.00-$75.00

Plate 402 . . . . $40.00-$50.00

Plate 403 . . . . . $40.00-$50.00

Plate 404 . . . . . $60.00-$80.00

Plate 405 . . . $80.00-$100.00

Plate 406 . . . . . $45.00-$55.00

Plate 407 . . . . . $55.00-$65.00

Plate 408 . . . . . $65.00-$75.00

Plate 409 . . . . . $55.00-$65.00

Plate 410 . . . . . $30.00-$40.00

Plate 411 . . . . . $45.00-$55.00

Plate 412 . . . . . $70.00-$80.00

Plate 413 . . . . . $50.00-$60.00

Plate 414 . . . $120.00-$140.00

Plate 415 . . . $120.00-$130.00

Plate 416 . . . $140.00-$160.00

Plate 417 . . . . $80.00-$100.00

Plate 418 . . . $150.00-$175.00

Plate 419 . . . . . $20.00-$25.00

Plate 420 . . . $150.00-$175.00

Plate 421 . . . . . $60.00-$80.00

Plate 422 . . . . . $20.00-$25.00

Plate 423 . . . $275.00-$325.00

Plate 424 . . . . . $60.00-$70.00

Plate 425 . . . $160.00-$180.00

Plate 426 . . . $80.00-$100.00

Plate 427 . . . . $80.00-$100.00

Plate 428 . . . . . $45.00-$55.00

Plate 429 . . . . . $30.00-$40.00

Plate 430 . . . $150.00-$175.00

Plate 431 . . . $200.00-$250.00

Plate 432 . . . $100.00-$125.00

Plate 433 . . . $100.00-$125.00

Bibliography

Barber, William Atlee. *Marks of American Potters*, 1904.

Boger, Louise Ade. *The Dictionary of World Pottery and Porcelain.* New York: Charles Scribner's Sons, 1971.

Brink, Mrs. William, "Staffordshire," *The Encyclopedia of Collectibles*. Alexandria, Virginia: Time-Life Books, 1980.

Copeland, Robert. *Spode's Willow Pattern and other Designs after the Chinese.* New York: Rizzoli, 1980.

Coysh, A.W. *Blue and White Transfer Ware 1780-1840*. Rutland, Vermont: Charles E. Tuttle Company, 1971.

Cushion, J.P. *Handbook of Pottery and Porcelain Marks*. London: Faber and Faber, 1980.

Fisher, S.W. *English Pottery and Porcelain Marks*. Des Moines, Iowa: Wallace-Homestead Book Co., 1970.

Gaston, Mary Frank. *The Collector's Encyclopedia of Limoges Porcelain*. Paducah, Kentucky: Collector Books, 1980.

_____. *Blue Willow, An Illustrated Value Guide*. Paducah, Kentucky: Collector Books, 1983.

Godden, Geoffrey A. *Encyclopedia of British Pottery and Porcelain Marks*. New York: Crown Publishers, 1964.

Hughes, G. Bernard. *The Collector's Pocket Book of China*. New York: Tandem Books, 1965.

_____. *English and Scottish Earthenware*. London: Abbey Fine Arts, n.d.

Hughes, Bernard and Therle. *The Collector's Encyclopaedia of English Ceramics*. London: Abbey Library, 1968.

Kovel, Ralph M. and Terry H. *Dictionary of Marks*. New York: Crown Publishers, Inc., 1953.

Lehner, Lois. *Ohio Pottery and Glass*. Des Moines, Iowa: Wallace-Homestead Book Co., 1978.

Little, W.L. *Staffordshire Blue*. London: B.T. Batsford, Ltd., 1969.

Mankowitz, Wolf and Reginald G. Haggar. *The Concise Encyclopedia of English Pottery and Porcelain*. New York: Hawthorn Books, Inc., n.d.

Mason, Veneita. *Popular Patterns of Flow Blue China with Prices*. Des Moines, Iowa: Wallace-Homestead Book Company, 1982.

Mountfield, David. *The Antique Collectors' Illustrated Dictionary*. London: Hamlyn, 1974.

Norbury, James. *The World of Victoriana*. London, Hamlyn, 1972.

Poche, Emanuel. *Porcelain Marks of the World*. New York: Arco Publishing Company, Inc., 1974.

Sandon, Henry. *Royal Worcester Porcelain from 1862 to the Present Day*. London: Barrie & Jenkins, 1973.

Williams, Petra. *Flow Blue China An Aid to Identification*. Jeffersontown, Kentucky: Fountain House East, 1971.

_____. *Flow Blue China II*. Jeffersontown, Kentucky: Fountain House East, 1973.

_____. *Flow Blue China and Mulberry Ware*. Jeffersontown, Kentucky: Fountain House East, 1975.